There Was a Time

Edward Thomas

A Phoenix Paperback

This edition published in 1996 by Phoenix,
a division of Orion Books Ltd,
Orion House, 5 Upper St Martin's Lane, London WC2H 9EA

ISBN 1 85799 676 3

Typeset by CentraCet Ltd, Cambridge
Printed in Great Britain by
Clays Ltd, St Ives plc

CONTENTS

The Sign Post

The dim sea glints chill. The white sun is shy,
And the skeleton weeds and the never-dry,
Rough, long grasses keep white with frost
At the hilltop by the finger-post;
The smoke of the traveller's-joy is puffed
Over hawthorn berry and hazel tuft.
I read the sign. Which way shall I go?
A voice says: You would not have doubted so
At twenty. Another voice gentle with scorn
Says: At twenty you wished you had never been
    born.

One hazel lost a leaf of gold
From a tuft at the tip, when the first voice told
The other he wished to know what 'twould be
To be sixty by this same post. 'You shall see,'
He laughed – and I had to join his laughter –
'You shall see; but either before or after,
Whatever happens, it must befall,
A mouthful of earth to remedy all
Regrets and wishes shall freely be given;
And if there be a flaw in that heaven
'Twill be freedom to wish, and your wish may be

To be here or anywhere talking to me,
No matter what the weather, on earth,
At any age between death and birth, –
To see what day or night can be,
The sun and the frost, the land and the sea,
Summer, Autumn, Winter, Spring, –
With a poor man of any sort, down to a king,
Standing upright out in the air
Wondering where he shall journey, O where?'

The Manor Farm

The rock-like mud unfroze a little and rills
Ran and sparkled down each side of the road
Under the catkins wagging in the hedge.
But earth would have her sleep out, spite of the sun;
Nor did I value that thin gilding beam
More than a pretty February thing
Till I came down to the old Manor Farm,
And church and yew-tree opposite, in age
Its equals and in size. The church and yew
And farmhouse slept in a Sunday silentness.
The air raised not a straw. The steep farm roof,
With tiles duskily glowing, entertained
The mid-day sun; and up and down the roof
White pigeons nestled. There was no sound but one.
Three cart-horses were looking over a gate

Drowsily through their forelocks, swishing their
    tails
Against a fly, a solitary fly.

The Winter's cheek flushed as if he had drained
Spring, Summer, and Autumn at a draught
And smiled quietly. But 'twas not Winter –
Rather a season of bliss unchangeable
Awakened from farm and church where it had lain
Safe under tile and thatch for ages since
This England, Old already, was called Merry.

The Owl

Downhill I came hungry, and yet not starved;
Cold, yet had heat within me that was proof
Against the North wind; tired, yet so that rest
Had seemed the sweetest thing under a roof.

Then at the inn I had food, fire, and rest,
Knowing how hungry, cold, and tired was I.
All of the night was quite barred out except
An owl's cry, a most melancholy cry

Shaken out long and clear upon the hill,
No merry note, nor cause of merriment,

But one telling me plain what I escaped
And others could not, that night, as in I went.

And salted was my food, and my repose,
Salted and sobered, too, by the bird's voice
Speaking for all who lay under the stars,
Soldiers and poor, unable to rejoice.

As the Team's Head-Brass

As the team's head-brass flashed out on the turn
The lovers disappeared into the wood.
I sat among the boughs of the fallen elm
That strewed the angle of the fallow, and
Watched the plough narrowing a yellow square
Of charlock. Every time the horses turned
Instead of treading me down, the ploughman leaned
Upon the handles to say or ask a word,
About the weather, next about the war.
Scraping the share he faced towards the wood,
And screwed along the furrow till the brass flashed
Once more.
              The blizzard felled the elm whose crest
I sat in, by a woodpecker's round hole,
The ploughman said. 'When will they take it away?'
'When the war's over.' So the talk began
One minute and an interval of ten,

A minute more and the same interval.
'Have you been out?' 'No.' 'And don't want to,
    perhaps?'
'If I could only come back again, I should.
I could spare an arm. I shouldn't want to lose
A leg. If I should lose my head, why, so,
I should want nothing more . . . Have many gone
From here?' 'Yes.' 'Many lost?' 'Yes, a good few.
Only two teams work on the farm this year.
One of my mates is dead. The second day
In France they killed him. It was back in March,
The very night of the blizzard, too. Now if
He had stayed here we should have moved the tree.'
'And I should not have sat here. Everything
Would have been different. For it would have been
Another world.' 'Ay, and a better, though
If we could see all all might seem good.' Then
The lovers came out of the wood again:
The horses started and for the last time
I watched the clods crumble and topple over
After the ploughshare and the stumbling team.

Like the Touch of Rain

Like the touch of rain she was
On a man's flesh and hair and eyes
When the joy of walking thus
Has taken him by surprise:

With the love of the storm he burns,
He sings, he laughs, well I know how,
But forgets when he returns
As I shall not forget her 'Go now'.

Those two words shut a door
Between me and the blessed rain
That was never shut before
And will not open again.

The Path

Running along a bank, a parapet
That saves from the precipitous wood below
The level road, there is a path. It serves
Children for looking down the long smooth steep,
Between the legs of beech and yew, to where
A fallen tree checks the sight: while men and women

Content themselves with the road and what they see
Over the bank, and what the children tell.
The path, winding like silver, trickles on,
Bordered and even invaded by thinnest moss
That tries to cover roots and crumbling chalk
With gold, olive, and emerald, but in vain
The children wear it. They have flattened the bank
On top, and silvered it between the moss
With the current of their feet, year after year.
But the road is houseless, and leads not to school.
To see a child is rare there, and the eye
Has but the road, the wood that overhangs
And underyawns it, and the path that looks
As if it led on to some legendary
Or fancied place where men have wished to go
And stay; till, sudden, it ends where the wood ends.

If I Should Ever by Chance

If I should ever by chance grow rich
I'll buy Codham, Cockridden, and Childerditch,
Roses, Pyrgo, and Lapwater,
And let them all to my elder daughter.
The rent I shall ask of her will be only
Each year's first violets, white and lonely,
The first primroses and orchises –
She must find them before I do, that is.

But if she finds a blossom on furze
Without rent they shall all for ever be hers,
Whenever I am sufficiently rich:
Codham, Cockridden, and Childerditch,
Roses, Pyrgo and Lapwater, –
I shall give them all to my elder daughter.

What Shall I Give?

What shall I give my daughter the younger
More than will keep her from cold and hunger?
I shall not give her anything.
If she shared South Weald and Havering,
Their acres, the two brooks running between,
Paine's Brook and Weald Brook,
With pewit, woodpecker, swan, and rook,
She would be no richer than the queen
Who once on a time sat in Havering Bower
Alone, with the shadows, pleasure and power.
She could do no more with Samarcand,
Or the mountains of a mountain land
And its far white house above cottages
Like Venus above the Pleiades.
Her small hands I would not cumber
With so many acres and their lumber,
But leave her Steep and her own world
And her spectacled self with hair uncurled,

Wanting a thousand little things
That time without contentment brings.

When First

When first I came here I had hope,
Hope for I knew not what. Fast beat
My heart at sight of the tall slope
Of grass and yews, as if my feet

Only by scaling its steps of chalk
Would see something no other hill
Ever disclosed. And now I walk
Down it the last time. Never will

My heart beat so again at sight
Of any hill although as fair
And loftier. For infinite
The change, late unperceived, this year,

The twelfth, suddenly, shows me plain.
Hope now, – not health, nor cheerfulness,
Since they can come and go again,
As often one brief hour witnesses, –

Just hope has gone for ever. Perhaps
I may love other hills yet more

Than this: the future and the maps
Hide something I was waiting for.

One thing I know, that love with chance
And use and time and necessity
Will grow, and louder the heart's dance
At parting than at meeting be.

When We Two Walked

When we two walked in Lent
We imagined that happiness
Was something different
And this was something less.

But happy were we to hide
Our happiness, not as they were
Who acted in their pride
Juno and Jupiter:

For the Gods in their jealousy
Murdered that wife and man,
And we that were wise live free
To recall our happiness then.

Early One Morning

Early one morning in May I set out,
And nobody I knew was about.
    I'm bound away for ever,
     Away somewhere, away for ever.

There was no wind to trouble the weathercocks.
I had burnt my letters and darned my socks.

No one knew I was going away,
I thought myself I should come back some day.

I heard the brook through the town gardens run.
O sweet was the mud turned to dust by the sun.

A gate banged in a fence and banged in my head.
'A fine morning, sir,' a shepherd said.

I could not return from my liberty,
To my youth and my love and my misery.

The past is the only dead thing that smells sweet,
The only sweet thing that is not also fleet.
    I'm bound away for ever,
     Away somewhere, away for ever.

The Huxter

He has a hump like an ape on his back;
He has of money a plentiful lack;
And but for a gay coat of double his girth
There is not a plainer thing on the earth
     This fine May morning.

But the huxter has a bottle of beer;
He drives a cart and his wife sits near
Who does not heed his lack or his hump;
And they laugh as down the lane they bump
     This fine May morning.

Lob

At hawthorn-time in Wiltshire travelling
In search of something chance would never bring,
An old man's face, by life and weather cut
And coloured, – rough, brown, sweet as any nut, –
A land face, sea-blue-eyed, – hung in my mind
When I had left him many a mile behind.
All he said was: 'Nobody can't stop 'ee. It's
A footpath, right enough. You see those bits
Of mounds – that's where they opened up the barrows
Sixty years since, while I was scaring sparrows.

They thought as there was something to find there,
But couldn't find it, by digging, anywhere.'

To turn back then and seek him, where was the use?
There were three Manningfords, – Abbots, Bohun, and
      Bruce:
And whether Alton, not Manningford, it was,
My memory could not decide, because
There was both Alton Barnes and Alton Priors.
All had their churches, graveyards, farms, and byres,
Lurking to one side up the paths and lanes,
Seldom well seen except by aeroplanes;
And when bells rang, or pigs squealed, or cocks crowed,
Then only heard. Ages ago the road
Approached. The people stood and looked and turned.
Nor asked it to come nearer, nor yet learned
To move out there and dwell in all men's dust.
And yet withal they shot the weathercock, just
Because 'twas he crowed out of tune, they said:
So now the copper weathercock is dead.
If they had reaped their dandelions and sold
Them fairly, they could have afforded gold.

Many years passed, and I went back again
Among those villages, and looked for men
Who might have known my ancient. He himself
Had long been dead or laid upon the shelf,
I thought. One man I asked about him roared

At my description: 'Tis old Bottlesford
He means, Bill.' But another said: 'Of course,
It was Jack Button up at the White Horse.
He's dead, sir, these three years.' This lasted till
A girl proposed Walker of Walker's Hill,
'Old Adam Walker. Adam's Point you'll see
Marked on the maps.'

                                    'That was her roguery.'
The next man said. He was a squire's son
Who loved wild bird and beast, and dog and gun
For killing them. He had loved them from his birth,
One with another, as he loved the earth.
'The man may be like Button, or Walker, or
Like Bottlesford, that you want, but far more
He sounds like one I saw when I was a child.
I could almost swear to him. The man was wild
And wandered. His home was where he was free.
Everybody has met one such man as he.
Does he keep clear old paths that no one uses
But once a lifetime when he loves or muses?
He is English as this gate, these flowers, this mire.
And when at eight years old Lob-lie-by-the-fire
Came in my books, this was the man I saw.
He has been in England as long as dove and daw,
Calling the wild cherry tree the merry tree,
The rose campion Bridget-in-her-bravery;
And in a tender mood he, as I guess,

Christened one flower Love-in-idleness,
And while he walked from Exeter to Leeds
One April called all cuckoo-flowers Milkmaids.
From him old herbal Gerard learnt, as a boy,
To name wild clematis the Traveller's-joy.
Our blackbirds sang no English till his ear
Told him they called his Jan Toy "Pretty dear".
(She was Jan Toy the Lucky, who, having lost
A shilling, and found a penny loaf, rejoiced.)
For reasons of his own to him the wren
Is Jenny Pooter. Before all other men
'Twas he first called the Hog's Back the Hog's Back.
That Mother Dunch's Buttocks should not lack
Their name was his care. He too could explain
Totteridge and Totterdown and Juggler's Lane:
He knows, if anyone. Why Tumbling Bay,
Inland in Kent, is called so, he might say.

'But little he says compared with what he does.
If ever a sage troubles him he will buzz
Like a beehive to conclude the tedious fray:
And the sage, who knows all languages, runs away.
Yet Lob has thirteen hundred names for a fool,
And though he never could spare time for school
To unteach what the fox so well expressed,
On biting the cock's head off, – Quietness is best, –
He can talk quite as well as anyone
After his thinking is forgot and done.   15

He first of all told someone else's wife,
For a farthing she'd skin a flint and spoil a knife
Worth sixpence skinning it. She heard him speak:
"She had a face as long as a wet week"
Said he, telling the tale in after years.
With blue smock and with gold rings in his ears,
Sometimes he is a pedlar, not too poor
To keep his wit. This is tall Tom that bore
The logs in, and with Shakespeare in the hall
Once talked, when icicles hung by the wall.
As Herne the Hunter he has known hard times.
On sleepless nights he made up weather rhymes
Which others spoilt. And, Hob being then his name,
He kept the hog that thought the butcher came
To bring his breakfast. "You thought wrong", said Hob.
When there were kings in Kent this very Lob,
Whose sheep grew fat and he himself grew merry,
Wedded the king's daughter of Canterbury;
For he alone, unlike squire, lord, and king,
Watched a night by her without slumbering;
He kept both waking. When he was but a lad
He won a rich man's heiress, deaf, dumb, and sad,
By rousing her to laugh at him. He carried
His donkey on his back. So they were married.
And while he was a little cobbler's boy
He tricked the giant coming to destroy
Shrewsbury by flood, "And how far is it yet?"
The giant asked in passing, "I forget;

But see these shoes I've worn out on the road
and we're not there yet." He emptied out his load
Of shoes for mending. The giant let fall from his spade
The earth for damming the Severn, and thus made
The Wreckin hill; and little Ercall hill
Rose where the giant scraped his boots. While still
So young, our Jack was chief of Gotham's sages.
But long before he could have been wise, ages
Earlier than this, while he grew thick and strong
And ate his bacon, or, at times, sang a song
And merely smelt it, as Jack the giant-killer
He made a name. He too ground up the miller,
The Yorkshireman who ground men's bones for flour.

'Do you believe Jack dead before his hour?
Or that his name is Walker, or Bottlesford,
Or Button, a mere clown, or squire, or lord?
The man you saw, – Lob-lie-by-the-fire, Jack Cade,
Jack Smith, Jack Moon, poor Jack of every trade,
Young Jack, or old Jack, or Jack What-d'ye-call,
Jack-in-the-hedge, or Robin-run-by-the-wall,
Robin Hood, Ragged Robin, lazy Bob,
One of the lords of No Man's Land, good Lob, –
Although he was seen dying at Waterloo,
Hastings, Agincourt, and Sedgemoor too, –
Lives yet. He never will admit he is dead
Till millers cease to grind men's bones for bread,
Not till our weathercock crows once again

And I remove my house out of the lane
On to the road.' With this he disappeared
In hazel and thorn tangled with old-man's-beard.
But one glimpse of his back, as there he stood,
Choosing his way, proved him of old Jack's blood,
Young Jack perhaps, and now a Wiltshireman
As he has oft been since his days began.

Some Eyes Condemn

Some eyes condemn the earth they gaze upon:
Some wait patiently till they know far more
Than earth can tell them: some laugh at the whole
As folly of another's making: one
I knew that laughed because he saw, from core
To rind, not one thing worth the laugh his soul
Had ready at waking: some eyes have begun
With laughing; some stand startled at the door.

Others, too, I have seen rest, question, roll,
Dance, shoot. And many I have loved watching.
    Some
I could not take my eyes from till they turned
And loving died. I had not found my goal.
But thinking of your eyes, dear, I become
Dumb: for they flamed and it was me they burned.

The Glory

The glory of the beauty of the morning, –
The cuckoo crying over the untouched dew;
The blackbird that has found it, and the dove
That tempts me on to something sweeter than love;
White clouds ranged even and fair as new-mown hay;
The heat, the stir, the sublime vacancy
Of sky and meadow and forest and my own heart: –
The glory invites me, yet it leaves me scorning
All I can ever do, all I can be,
Beside the lovely of motion, shape, and hue,
The happiness I fancy fit to dwell
In beauties presence. Shall I now this day
Begin to seek as far as heaven, as hell,
Wisdom or strength to match this beauty start
And tread the pale dust pitted with small dark drops,
In hope to find whatever it is I seek,
Hearkening to short-lived happy-seeming things
That we know naught of, in the hazel copse?
Or must I be content with discontent
As larks and swallows are perhaps with wings?
And shall I ask at the day's end once more
What beauty is, and what I can have meant
By happiness? And shall I let all go,
Glad, weary, or both? Or shall I perhaps know
That I was happy oft and oft before,

Awhile forgetting how I am fast pent,
How dreary-swift, with naught to travel to,
Is Time? I cannot bite the day to the core.

Adlestrop

Yes. I remember Adlestrop –
The name, because one afternoon
Of heat the express-train drew up there
Unwontedly. It was late June.

The steam hissed. Someone cleared his throat.
No one left and no one came
On the bare platform. What I saw
Was Adlestrop – only the name

And willows, willow-herb, and grass,
And meadowsweet, and haycocks dry,
No whit less still and lonely fair
Than the high cloudlets in the sky.

And for that minute a blackbird sang
Close by, and round him, mistier,
Farther and farther, all the birds
Of Oxfordshire and Gloucestershire.

Tall Nettles

Tall nettles cover up, as they have done
These many springs, the rusty harrow, the plough
Long worn out, and the roller made of stone:
Only the elm butt tops the nettles now.

This corner of the farmyard I like most:
As well as any bloom upon a flower
I like the dust on the nettles, never lost
Except to prove the sweetness of a shower.

Liberty

The last light has gone out of the world, except
This moonlight lying on the grass like frost
Beyond the brink of the tall elm's shadow.
It is as if everything else had slept
Many an age, unforgotten and lost –
The men that were, the things done, long ago,
All I have thought; and but the moon and I
Live yet and here stand idle over a grave
Where all is buried. Both have liberty
To dream what we could do if we were free
To do some thing we had desired long,
The moon and I. There's none less free than who

Does nothing and has nothing else to do,
Being free only for what is not to his mind,
And nothing is to his mind. If every hour
Like this one passing that I have spent among
The wiser others when I have forgot
To wonder whether I was free or not,
Were piled before me, and not lost behind,
And I could take and carry them away
I should be rich; or if I had the power
To wipe out every one and not again
Regret, I should be rich to be so poor.
And yet I still am half in love with pain,
With what is imperfect, with both tears and mirth,
With things that have an end, with life and earth,
And this moon that leaves me dark within the
    door.

The Gallows

There was a weasel lived in the sun
  With all his family,
Till a keeper shot him with his gun
  And hung him up on a tree,
Where he swings in the wind and rain,
  In the sun and in the snow,
Without pleasure, without pain,
  On the dead oak tree bough.

There was a crow who was no sleeper,
But a thief and a murderer
Till a very late hour; and this keeper
Made him one of the things that were,
To hang and flap in rain and wind,
In the sun and in the snow.
There are no more sins to be sinned
On the dead oak tree bough.

There was a magpie, too,
Had a long tongue and a long tail;
He could both talk and do –
But what did that avail?
He, too, flaps in the wind and rain
Alongside weasel and crow,
Without pleasure, without pain,
On the dead oak tree bough.

And many other beasts
And birds, skin, bone, and feather,
Have been taken from their feasts
And hung up there together,
To swing and have endless leisure
In the sun and in the snow,
Without pain, without pleasure,
On the dead oak tree bough.

Birds' Nests

The summer nests uncovered by autumn wind,
Some torn, others dislodged, all dark,
Everyone sees them: low or high in tree,
Or hedge, or single bush, they hang like a mark.

Since there's no need of eyes to see them with
I cannot help a little shame
That I missed most, even at eye's level, till
The leaves blew off and made the seeing no game.

'Tis a light pang. I like to see the nests
Still in their places, now first known,
At home and by far roads. Boys knew them not,
Whatever jays and squirrels may have done.

And most I like the winter nests deep-hid
That leaves and berries fell into:
Once a dormouse dined there on hazel-nuts,
And grass and goose-grass seeds found soil and grew.

'Home'

Fair was the morning, fair our tempers, and
We had seen nothing fairer than that land,
Though strange, and the untrodden snow that made
Wild of the tame, casting out all that was
Not wild and rustic and old; and we were glad.

Fair too was afternoon, and first to pass
Were we that league of snow, next the north wind.

There was nothing to return for, except need,
And yet we sang nor ever stopped for speed,
As we did often with the start behind.
Faster still strode we when we came in sight
Of the cold roofs where we must spend the night.
Happy we had not been there, nor could be,
Though we had tasted sleep and food and fellowship
Together long.

       'How quick', to someone's lip
The words came, 'will the beaten horse run home!'

The word 'home' raised a smile in us all three,
And one repeated it, smiling just so
That all knew what he meant and none would say.
Between three counties far apart that lay

We were divided and looked strangely each
At the other, and we knew we were not friends
But fellows in a union that ends
With the necessity for it, as it ought.

Never a word was spoken, not a thought
Was thought, of what the look meant with the word
'Home' as we walked and watched the sunset blurred.
And then to me the word, only the word,
'Homesick', as it were playfully occurred:
No more.
         If I should ever more admit
Than the mere word I could not endure it
For a day longer: this captivity
Must somehow come to an end, else I should be
Another man, as often now I seem,
Or this life be only an evil dream.

Lights Out

I have come to the borders of sleep,
The unfathomable deep
Forest where all must lose
Their way, however straight,
Or winding, soon or late;
They cannot choose.

Many a road and track
That, since the dawn's first crack,
Up to the forest brink,
Deceived the travellers,
Suddenly now blurs,
And in they sink.

Here love ends,
Despair, ambition ends;
All pleasure and all trouble,
Although most sweet or bitter,
Here ends in sleep that is sweeter
Than tasks most noble.

There is not any book
Or face of dearest look
That I would not turn from now
To go into the unknown
I must enter, and leave, alone,
I know not how.

The tall forest towers;
Its cloudy foliage lowers
Ahead, shelf above shelf;
Its silence I hear and obey
That I may lose my way
And myself.

Words

Out of us all
That make rhymes,
Will you choose
Sometimes –
As the winds use
A crack in a wall
Or a drain,
Their joy or their pain
To whistle through –
Choose me,
You English words?

I know you:
You are light as dreams,
Tough as oak,
Precious as gold,
As poppies and corn,
Or an old cloak:
Sweet as our birds
To the ear,
As the burnet rose
In the heat
Of Midsummer:
Strange as the races
Of dead and unborn:

Strange and sweet
Equally,
And familiar,
To the eye,
As the dearest faces
That a man knows,
And as lost homes are:
But though older far
Than oldest yew, –
As our hills are, old, –
Worn new
Again and again:
Young as our streams
After rain:
And as dear
As the earth which you prove
That we love.

Make me content
With some sweetness
From Wales
Whose nightingales
Have no wings, –
From Wiltshire and Kent
And Herefordshire,
And the villages there, –
From the names, and the things
No less.

Let me sometimes dance
With you,
Or climb
Or stand perchance
In ecstasy,
Fixed and free
In a rhyme,
As poets do.

February Afternoon

Men heard this roar of parleying starlings, saw,
   A thousand years ago even as now,
   Black rooks with white gulls following the plough
So that the first are last until a caw
Commands that last are first again, – a law
   Which was of old when one, like me, dreamed how
   A thousand years might dust lie on his brow
Yet thus would birds do between hedge and shaw.

Time swims before me, making as a day
   A thousand years, while the broad ploughland oak
   Roars mill-like and men strike and bear the stroke
   Of war as ever, audacious or resigned,
And God still sits aloft in the array
   That we have wrought him, stone-deaf and stone-
     blind.

Digging

What matter makes my spade for tears or mirth,
Letting down two clay pipes into the earth?
The one I smoked, the other a soldier
Of Blenheim, Ramillies, and Malplaquet
Perhaps. The dead man's immortality
Lies represented lightly with my own,
A yard or two nearer the living air
Than bones of ancients who, amazed to see
Almighty God erect the mastodon,
Once laughed, or wept, in this same light of day.

To-Night

Harry, you know at night
The larks in Castle Alley
Sing from the attic's height
As if the electric light
Were the true sun above a summer valley:
Whistle, don't knock, to-night.

I shall come early, Kate:
And we in Castle Alley
Will sit close out of sight
Alone, and ask no light

Of lamp or sun above a summer valley:
To-night I can stay late.

She Dotes

She dotes on what the wild birds say
Or hint or mock at, night and day, –
Thrush, blackbird, all that sing in May,
    And songless plover,
Hawk, heron, owl, and woodpecker.
They never say a word to her
    About her lover.

She laughs at them for childishness,
She cries at them for carelessness
Who see her going loverless
    Yet sing and chatter
Just as when he was not a ghost,
Nor ever ask her what she has lost
    Or what is the matter.

Yet she has fancied blackbirds hide
A secret, and that thrushes chide
Because she thinks death can divide
    Her from her lover:
And she has slept, trying to translate

The word the cuckoo cries to his mate
  Over and over.

Over the Hills

Often and often it came back again
To mind, the day I passed the horizon ridge
To a new country, the path I had to find
By half-gaps that were stiles once in the hedge,
The pack of scarlet clouds running across
The harvest evening that seemed endless then
And after, and the inn where all were kind,
All were strangers. I did not know my loss
Till one day twelve months later suddenly
I leaned upon my spade and saw it all,
Though far beyond the sky-line. It became
Almost a habit through the year for me
To lean and see it and think to do the same
Again for two days and a night. Recall
Was vain: no more could the restless brook
Ever turn back and climb the waterfall
To the lake that rests and stirs not in its nook,
As in the hollow of the collar-bone
Under the mountain's head of rush and stone.

Digging

To-day I think
Only with scents, – scents dead leaves yield,
And bracken, and wild carrot's seed,
And the square mustard field;

Odours that rise
When the spade wounds the root of tree,
Rose, currant, raspberry, or goutweed,
Rhubarb or celery;

The smoke's smell, too,
Flowing from where a bonfire burns
The dead, the waste, the dangerous,
And all to sweetness turns.

It is enough
To smell, to crumble the dark earth,
While the robin sings over again
Sad songs of Autumn mirth.

But These Things Also

But these things also are Spring's –
On banks by the roadside the grass
Long-dead that is greyer now
Than all the Winter it was;

The shell of a little snail bleached
In the grass; chip of flint, and mite
Of chalk; and the small birds' dung
In splashes of purest white:

All the white things a man mistakes
For earliest violets
Who seeks through Winter's ruins
Something to pay Winter's debts,

While the North blows, and starling flocks
By chattering on and on
Keep their spirits up in the mist,
And Spring's here, Winter's not gone.

Lovers

The two men in the road were taken aback.
The lovers came out shading their eyes from the sun,
And never was white so white, or black so black,
As her cheeks and hair. 'There are more things than one
A man might turn into a wood for, Jack,'
Said George; Jack whispered: 'He has not got a gun.
It's a bit too much of a good thing, I say.
They are going the other road, look. And see her run.' –
She ran. – 'What a thing it is, this picking may!'

The Word

There are so many things I have forgot,
That once were much to me, or that were not,
All lost, as is a childless woman's child
And its child's children, in the undefiled
Abyss of what will never be again.
I have forgot, too, names of the mighty men
That fought and lost or won in the old wars,
Of kings and fiends and gods, and most of the stars.
Some things I have forgot that I forget.
But lesser things there are, remembered yet,
Than all the others. One name that I have not –
Though 'tis an empty thingless name – forgot

Never can die because Spring after Spring
Some thrushes learn to say it as they sing.
There is always one at midday saying it clear
And tart – the name, only the name I hear.
While perhaps I am thinking of the elder scent
That is like food; or while I am content
With the wild rose scent that is like memory,
This name suddenly is cried out to me
From somewhere in the bushes by a bird
Over and over again, a pure thrush word.

Aspens

All day and night, save winter, every weather,
Above the inn, the smithy, and the shop,
The aspens at the cross-roads talk together
Of rain, until their last leaves fall from the top.

Out of the blacksmith's cavern comes the ringing
Of hammer, shoe, and anvil; out of the inn
The clink, the hum, the roar, the random singing –
The sounds that for these fifty years have been.

The whisper of the aspens is not drowned,
And over lightless pane and footless road,
Empty as sky, with every other sound
Not ceasing, calls their ghosts from their abode,

A silent smithy, a silent inn, nor hails
In the bare moonlight or the thick-furred gloom,
In tempest or the night of nightingales,
To turn the cross-roads to a ghostly room.

And it would be the same were no house near.
Over all sorts of weather, men, and times,
Aspens must shake their leaves and men may hear
But need not listen, more than to my rhymes.

Whatever wind blows while they and I have leaves
We cannot other than an aspen be
That ceaselessly, unreasonably grieves,
Or so men think who like a different tree.

An Old Song

I was not apprenticed nor ever dwelt in famous
    Lincolnshire;
I've served one master ill and well much more than seven
    year;
And never took up to poaching as you shall quickly find;
    But 'tis my delight of a shiny night in the season of the
    year.

I roamed where nobody had a right but keepers and
    squires, and there

I sought for nests, wild flowers, oak sticks, and moles,
    both far and near.
And had to run from farmers, and learnt the
    Lincolnshire song:
  'Oh, 'tis my delight of a shiny night in the season of
    the year.'

I took those walks years after, walking with friend or
    dear,
Or solitary musing; but when the moon shone clear
I had no joy or sorrow that could not be expressed
  By ''Tis my delight of a shiny night in the season of
    the year.'

Since then I've thrown away a chance to fight a
    gamekeeper;
And I less often trespass, and what I see or hear
Is mostly from the road or path by day: yet still I sing:
  'Oh, 'tis my delight of a shiny night in the season of
    the year.'

For if I am contented, at home or anywhere,
Or if I sigh for I know not what, or my heart beats with
    some fear,
It is a strange kind of delight to sing or whistle just:
  'Oh, 'tis my delight of a shiny night in the season of
    the year.'

And with this melody on my lips and no one by to care,
Indoors, or out on shiny nights or dark in open air,
I am for a moment made a man that sings out of his
  heart:
  'Oh, 'tis my delight of a shiny night in the season of
    the year.'

There Was a Time

There was a time when this poor frame was whole
And I had youth and never another care,
Or none that should have troubled a strong soul.
Yet, except sometimes in a frosty air
When my heels hammered out a melody
From pavements of a city left behind,
I never would acknowledge my own glee
Because it was less mighty than my mind
Had dreamed of. Since I could not boast of strength
Great as I wished, weakness was all my boast.
I sought yet hated pity till at length
I earned it. Oh, too heavy was the cost!
But now that there is something I could use
My youth and strength for, I deny the age,
The care and weakness that I know – refuse
To admit I am unworthy of the wage
Paid to a man who gives up eyes and breath
For what would neither ask nor heed his death.

No One Cares Less than I

'No one cares less than I,
Nobody knows but God,
Whether I am destined to lie
Under a foreign clod,'
Were the words I made to the bugle call in the morning.

But laughing, storming, scorning,
Only the bugles know
What the bugles say in the morning,
And they do not care, when they blow
The call that I heard and made words to early this
        morning.

Roads

I love roads:
The goddesses that dwell
Far along invisible
Are my favourite gods.

Roads go on
While we forget, and are
Forgotten like a star
That shoots and is gone.

On this earth 'tis sure
We men have not made
Anything that doth fade
So soon, so long endure:

The hill road wet with rain
In the sun would not gleam
Like a winding stream
If we trod it not again.

They are lonely
While we sleep, lonelier
For lack of the traveller
Who is now a dream only.

From dawn's twilight
And all the clouds like sheep
On the mountains of sleep
They wind into the night.

The next turn may reveal
Heaven: upon the crest
The close pine clump, at rest
And black, may Hell conceal.

Often footsore, never
Yet of the road I weary,

Though long and steep and dreary,
As it winds on for ever.

Helen of the roads,
The mountain ways of Wales
And the Mabinogion tales
Is one of the true gods,

Abiding in the trees,
The threes and fours so wise,
The larger companies,
That by the roadside be,

And beneath the rafter
Else uninhabited
Excepting by the dead;
And it is her laughter

At morn and night I hear
When the thrush cock sings
Bright irrelevant things,
And when the chanticleer

Calls back to their own night
Troops that make loneliness
With their light footsteps' press,
As Helen's own are light.

Now all roads lead to France
And heavy is the tread
Of the living; but the dead
Returning lightly dance:

Whatever the road bring
To me or take from me,
They keep me company
With their pattering.

Crowding the solitude
Of the loops over the downs,
Hushing the roar of towns
And their brief multitude.

The Chalk-Pit

'Is this the road that climbs above and bends
Round what was once a chalk-pit: now it is
By accident an amphitheatre.
Some ash trees standing ankle-deep in briar
And bramble act the parts, and neither speak
Nor stir,' 'But see: they have fallen, every one,
And briar and bramble have grown over them.'
'That is the place. As usual no one is here.
Hardly can I imagine the drop of the axe,
And the smack that is like an echo, sounding here.'

'I do not understand.' 'Why, what I mean is
That I have seen the place two or three times
At most, and that its emptiness and silence
And stillness haunt me, as if just before
It was not empty, silent, still, but full
Of life of some kind, perhaps tragical.
Has anything unusual happened here?'
'Not that I know of. It is called the Dell.
They have not dug chalk here for a century.
That was the ash trees' age. But I will ask.'
'No. Do not. I prefer to make a tale,
Or better leave it like the end of a play,
Actors and audience and lights all gone;
For so it looks now. In my memory
Again and again I see it, strangely dark,
And vacant of a life but just withdrawn.
We have not seen the woodman with the axe.
Some ghost has left it now as we two came,'
'And yet you doubted if this were the road?'
'Well, sometimes I have thought of it and failed
To place it. No. And I am not quite sure,
Even now, this is it. For another place,
Real or painted, may have combined with it.
Or I myself a long way back in time . . .'
'Why, as to that, I used to meet a man –
I had forgotten, – searching for birds' nests
Along the road and in the chalk-pit too.
The wren's hole was an eye that looked at him

For recognition. Every nest he knew.
He got a stiff neck, by looking this side or that,
Spring after spring, he told me, with his laugh, –
A sort of laugh. He was a visitor,
A man of forty, – smoked and strolled about.
At orts and crosses Pleasure and Pain had played
On his brown features; – I think both had lost; –
Mild and yet wild too. You may know the kind.
And once or twice a woman shared his walks,
A girl of twenty with a brown boy's face,
And hair brown as a thrush or as a nut,
Thick eyebrows, glinting eyes – ' 'You have said enough.
A pair, – free thought, free love, – I know the breed:
I shall not mix my fancies up with them.'
'You please yourself. I should prefer the truth
Or nothing. Here, in fact, is nothing at all
Except a silent place that once rang loud,
And trees and us – imperfect friends, we men
And trees since time began; and nevertheless
Between us still we breed a mystery.'

Beauty

What does it mean? Tired, angry, and ill at ease,
No man, woman, or child alive could please
Me now. And yet I almost dare to laugh
Because I sit and frame an epitaph –

'Here lies all that no one loved of him
And that loved no one.' Then in a trice that whim
Has wearied. But, though I am like a river
At fall of evening while it seems that never
Has the sun lighted it or warmed it, while
Cross breezes cut the surface to a file,
This heart, some fraction of me, happily
Floats through the window even now to a tree
Down in the misting, dim-lit, quiet vale,
Not like a pewit that returns to wail
For something it has lost, but like a dove
That slants unswerving to its home and love.
There I find my rest, and through the dusk air
Flies what yet lives in me. Beauty is there.

The New Year

He was the one man I met up in the woods
That stormy New Year's morning; and at first sight,
Fifty yards off, I could not tell how much
Of the strange tripod was a man. His body
Bowed horizontal, was supported equally
By legs at one end, by a rake at the other:
Thus he rested, far less like a man than
His wheel-barrow in profile was like a pig.
But when I saw it was an old man bent,
At the same moment came into my mind

The games at which boys bend thus, *High-cocolorum*,
Or *Fly-the-garter*, and *leap-frog*. At the sound
Of footsteps he began to straighten himself;
His head rolled under his cape like a tortoise's;
He took an unlit pipe out of his mouth
Politely ere I wished him 'A Happy New Year',
And with his head cast upward sideways muttered –
So far as I could hear through the trees' roar –
'Happy New Year, and may it come fastish, too,'
While I strode by and he turned to raking leaves.

The Other

The forest ended. Glad I was
To feel the light, and hear the hum
Of bees, and smell the drying grass
And the sweet mint, because I had come
To an end of forest, and because
Here was both road and inn, the sum
Of what's not forest. But 'twas here
They asked me if I did not pass
Yesterday this way. 'Not you? Queer.'
'Who then? and slept here?' I felt fear.

I leant his road and, ere they were
Sure I was I, left the dark wood
Behind, kestrel and woodpecker,

The inn in the sun, the happy mood
When first I tasted sunlight there.
I travelled fast, in hopes I should
Outrun that other. What to do
When caught, I planned not. I pursued
To prove the likeness, and, if true,
To watch until myself I knew.

I tried the inns that evening
Of a long gabled high-street grey,
Of courts and outskirts, travelling
And eager but a weary way,
In vain. He was not there. Nothing
Told me that ever till that day
Had one like me entered those doors,
Save once. That time I dared: 'You may
Recall' – but never-foamless shores
Make better friends than those dull
        boors.

Many and many a day like this
Aimed at the unseen moving goal
And nothing found but remedies
For all desire. These made not whole;
They sowed a new desire, a kiss
Desire's self beyond control,
Desire of desire. And yet
Life stayed on within my soul.

One night in sheltering from the wet
I quite forgot I could forget.

A customer, then the landlady
Stared at me. With a kind of smile
They hesitated awkwardly:
Their silence gave me time for guile.
Had anyone called there like me,
I asked. It was quite plain the wile
Succeeded. For they poured out all.
And that was naught. Less than a mile
Beyond the inn, I could recall
He was like me in general.

He had pleased them, but I less.
I was more eager than before
To find him out and to confess,
To bore him and to let him bore.
I could not wait: children might guess
I had a purpose, something more
That made an answer indiscreet.
One girl's caution made me sore,
Too indignant even to greet
That other had we chanced to meet.

I sought then in solitude.
The wind had fallen with the night; as still
The roads lay as the ploughland rude,

Dark and naked, on the hill.
Had there been ever any feud
'Twixt earth and sky, a mighty will
Closed it: the crocketed dark trees,
A dark house, dark impossible
Cloud-towers, one star, one lamp, one peace
Held on an everlasting lease:

And all was earth's, or all was sky's;
No difference endured between
The two. A dog barked on a hidden rise;
A marshbird whistled high unseen;
The latest waking blackbird's cries
Perished upon the silence keen.
The last light filled a narroiw firth
Among the clouds. I stood serene,
And with a solemn quiet mirth,
An old inhabitant of earth.

Once the name I gave to hours
Like this was melancholy, when
It was not happiness and powers
Coming like exiles home again,
And weaknesses quitting their bowers,
Smiled and enjoyed, far off from men,
Moments of everlastingness.
And fortunate my search was then

While what I sought, nevertheless,
That I was seeking, I did not guess.

That time was brief: once more at inn
And upon road I sought my man
Till once amid a tap-room's din
Loudly he asked for me, began
To speak, as if it had been a sin,
Of how I thought and dreamed and ran
After him thus, day after day:
He lived as one under a ban
For this: what had I got to say?
I said nothing. I slipped away.

And now I dare not follow after
Too close. I try to keep in sight,
Dreading his frown and worse his laughter.
I steal out of the wood to light;
I see the swift shoot from the rafter
By the inn door: ere I alight
I wait and hear the starlings wheeze
And nibble like ducks: I wait his flight.
He goes: I follow: no release
Until he ceases. Then I also shall cease.

The Gypsy

A fortnight before Christmas Gypsies were everywhere:
Vans were drawn up on wastes, women trailed to the
    fair.
'My gentleman,' said one, 'you've got a lucky face.'
'And you've a luckier,' I thought, 'if such a grace
And impudence in rags are lucky.' 'Give a penny
For the poor baby's sake.' 'Indeed I have not any
Unless you can give change for a sovereign, my dear.'
'Then just half a pipeful of tobacco can you spare?'
I gave it. With that much victory she laughed content.
I should have given more, but off and away she went
With her baby and her pink sham flowers to rejoin
The rest before I could translate to its proper coin
Gratitude for her grace. And I paid nothing then,
As I pay nothing now with the dipping of my pen
For her brother's music when he drummed the
    tambourine
And stamped his feet, which made the workmen passing
    grin,
While his mouth-organ changed to a rascally Bacchanal
    dance
'Over the hills and far away.' This and his glance
Outlasted all the fair, farmer, and auctioneer,
Cheap-jack, balloon-man, drover with crooked stick,
    and steer,

Pig, turkey, goose, and duck, Christmas corpses to be.
Not even the kneeling ox had eyes like the Romany.
That night he peopled for me the hollow wooded land,
More dark and wild than stormiest heavens, that I
    searched and scanned
Like a ghost new-arrived. The gradations of the dark
Were like an underworld of death, but for the spark
In the Gypsy boy's black eyes as he played and stamped
    his tune,
Over the hills and far away,' and a crescent moon.

Man and Dog

''Twill take some getting.' 'Sir, I think 'twill so.'
The old man stared up at the mistletoe
That hung too high in the poplar's crest for plunder
Of any climber, though not for kissing under:
Then he went on against the north-east wind –
Straight but lame, leaning on a staff new-skinned,
Carrying a brolly, flag-basket, and old coat, –
Towards Alton, ten miles off. And he had not
Done less from Chilgrove where he pulled up docks.
'Twere best, if he had had 'a money-box',
To have waited there till the sheep cleared a field
For what a half-week's flint-picking would yield.
His mind was running on the work he had done
Since he left Christchurch in the New Forest, one

Spring in the 'seventies, – navvying on dock and line
From Southampton to Newcastle-on-Tyne, –
In 'seventy-four a year of soldiering
With the Berkshires, – hoeing and harvesting
In half the shires where corn and couch will grow.
His sons, three sons, were fighting, but the hoe
And reap-hook he liked, or anything to do with trees.
He fell once from a poplar tall as these:
The Flying Man they called him in hospital.
'If I flew now, to another world I'd fall.'
He laughed and whistled to the small brown bitch
With spots of blue that hunted in the ditch.
Her foxy Welsh grandfather must have paired
Beneath him. He kept sheep in Wales and scared
Strangers, I will warrant, with his pearl eye
And trick of shrinking off as he were shy,
Then following close in silence for – for what?
'No rabbit, never fear, she ever got,
Yet always hunts. To-day she nearly had one:
She would and she wouldn't. 'Twas like that. The bad
    one!
She's not much use, but still she's company,
Though I'm not. She goes everywhere with me.
So Alton I must reach to-night somehow:
I'll get no shakedown with that bedfellow
From farmers. Many a man sleeps worse to-night
Than I shall.' 'In the trenches.' 'Yes, that's right.
But they'll be out of that – I hope they be –

This weather, marching after the enemy.'
'And so I hope. Good luck.' And there I nodded
'Good-night. You keep straight on,' Stiffly he plodded;
And at his heels the crisp leaves scurried fast,
And the leaf-coloured robin watched. They passed,
The robin till next day, the man for good,
Together in the twilight of the wood.

A Private

This ploughman dead in battle slept out of doors
Many a frozen night, and merrily
Answered staid drinkers, good bedmen, and all bores:
'At Mrs Greenland's Hawthorn Bush,' said he,
'I slept.' None knew which bush. Above the town,
Beyond 'The Drover', a hundred spot the down
In Wiltshire. And where now at last he sleeps
More sound in France – that, too, he secret keeps.

P.H.T.

I may come near loving you
When you are dead
And there is nothing to do
And much to be said.

To repent that day will be
Impossible
For you and vain for me
The truth to tell

I shall be sorry for
Your impotence:
You can do and undo no more
When you go hence,

Cannot even forgive
The funeral.
But not so long as you live
Can I love you at all.

Out in the Dark

Out in the dark over the snow
The fallow fawns invisible go
With the fallow doe;
And the winds blow
Fast as the stars are slow.

Stealthily the dark haunts round
And, when the lamp goes, without sound
At a swifter bound

Than the swiftest hound,
Arrives, and all else is drowned;

And star and I and wind and deer,
Are in the dark together, – near,
Yet far, – and fear
Drums on my ear
In that sage company drear.

How weak and little is the light,
All the universe of sight,
Love and delight,
Before the might,
If you love it not, of night.

A Note on Edward Thomas

Edward Thomas (1878–1917), the English poet and essayist, was born in London of Welsh parents. He was educated at St Paul's and Lincoln College, Oxford. His first book, *The Woodland Life*, appeared in 1897, and two years later, while still an undergraduate, he married Helen Noble. They lived in poverty in various parts of Kent while he tried to make a living by his books and by hack journalism. On the outbreak of the First World War he enlisted as a private and had received his commission as a second lieutenant when he was killed at Arras.

An intense love of the country is shown in his works, which include *Oxford*, 1903, *The Heart of England*, 1906, *The Country*, 1913, and *A Literary Pilgrim in England*, 1917. Thomas wrote no poetry until 1912, when he used the pseudonym Edward Eastaway; his *Collected Poems*, 1920, in a style limpid and precise, were praised by Walter de la Mare. *The Happy-Go-Lucky Morgans*, 1913, is a novel.

COLLINS GEM

BASIC FACTS

BIOLOGY

T A McCahill BSc DipEd MIBiol

HarperCollins*Publishers*

HarperCollins Publishers
PO Box, Glasgow G4 0NB, Scotland

First published 1982
Revised edition 1988
Third edition 1991

Reprint 10 9 8 7 6 5 4 3 2 1

ISBN 0 00 459114 3 (UK edition)
0 00 459115 1 (Export edition)

Printed in Great Britain by
HarperCollins Manufacturing, Glasgow

Introduction

Collins Gem *Basic Facts* is a series of illustrated GEM dictionaries in important school subjects. This new edition has been extensively revised and updated to widen the coverage of the subject and to reflect recent changes in the way it is taught in the classroom.

Bold words in an entry identify key terms which are explained in greater detail in entries of their own; important terms which do not have separate entries are shown in *italic* and are explained in the entry in which they occur.

Other titles in the series include:

Gem *Basic Facts Mathematics*
Gem *Basic Facts Chemistry*
Gem *Basic Facts Physics*
Gem *Basic Facts Science*
Gem *Basic Facts Computers*
Gem *Basic Facts History*
Gem *Basic Facts Geography*
Gem *Basic Facts Craft, Design & Technology*
Gem *Basic Facts Business Studies*

abdomen   1. In mammals, the part of the body separated from the **thorax** by the **diaphragm**, containing **stomach, liver, intestines**, etc.
2. In insects, the posterior third region of the body.

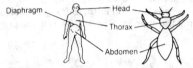

abdomen   The position of the abdomen in a human being and an insect.

abiotic factor   See **environment**.

abscission   The shedding of **leaves**, **fruit**, and unfertilized **flowers** from plants by the formation of a layer of cork **cells** which seal the plant surface and eventually cut off food and water from the part to be shed.

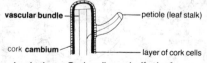

abscission   Cork cells seal off a leaf.

absorption (of food)   The process by which digested food particles pass from the **gut** into the bloodstream. In mammals absorption occurs in the **ileum**.

accommodation   The way in which the **eye** of mammals can change its sharp focus from near to distant objects, and vice-versa, by means of contraction or relaxation of the **ciliary muscles**, so altering the shape and hence the focusing proper-

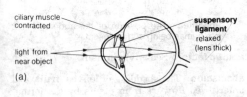

ciliary muscle contracted

suspensory ligament relaxed (lens thick)

light from near object

(a)

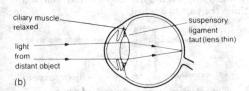

ciliary muscle relaxed

suspensory ligament taut (lens thin)

light from distant object

(b)

accommodation (a) eye focused on near object. (b) eye focused on distant object.

ties of the **lens**.

acid A substance which releases hydrogen **ions** in **water** and has a **pH** less than 7, e.g. hydrochloric acid in the human **stomach**.

active transport The movement of materials against a *concentration gradient* using **metabolic energy**.

Examples are (a) the uptake of **mineral salts** from **soil** by plant **root hairs** and (b) the re-absorption of certain substances by the mammalian **kidney**. See **diffusion**.

adaptation The development of structures within organisms so that they are more efficiently adapted to their **environment**, e.g. plant **leaves** are constructed in such a way as to contribute to the efficiency of **photosynthesis**.
Leaves are:
(a) thin, allowing rapid **diffusion** of air, thus facilitating **gas exchange**;
(b) flat and present a large surface area to the light. The **cells** immediately beneath the upper **epidermis** are called **palisade mesophyll** cells. They are closely packed and contain many **chloroplasts**, most of which are situated at the upper part of the cell, thus obtaining maximum light. Between the palisade cells and the lower epidermis are the

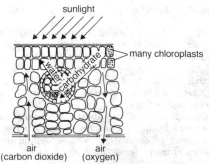

sunlight

many chloroplasts

air
(carbon dioxide)

air
(oxygen)

adaptation The structure of a leaf is adapted for efficient photosynthesis.

spongy mesophyll cells, which contain fewer chloroplasts. These cells are loosely packed, being separated by air spaces, which allow free circulation of air between the leaves and the atmosphere via the **stomata**.

The positioning of most of the stomata on the lower epidermis means that the important palisade layer is not interrupted by too many air spaces.

Water for photosynthesis is transported in **xylem** vessels in the mid-rib and veins, while the synthesised **carbohydrate** is transported throughout the plant via the **phloem** sieve tubes.

ADH See **antidiuretic hormone**.

adipose tissue Mammalian tissue consisting of **fat** storage **cells**, located under the **skin**, around the **kidneys**, etc.

adolescence The period in the human **life cycle** between **puberty** and maturity.

ADP See **ATP**.

adrenal glands A pair of **endocrine glands** situated anterior to the mammalian **kidneys** and secreting the **hormone** *adrenalin* which causes increased heart-beat, breathing, etc., in response to conditions of stress.

aerobe An organism which requires *oxygen* to survive. See **anaerobe**, **respiration**.

aerobic bacteria See **sewage disposal**.

agar A jelly obtained from seaweeds which is used as a medium for culturing **bacteria**. A food source, e.g. **glucose**, is added and the liquid agar is poured into a Petri dish where it solidifies. Bacterial sources are added to the *nutrient agar plate* and after two days at a suitable temperature (usually 37°C), the bacterial colonies become visible as a result of rapid cell division. See diagram on page 6.

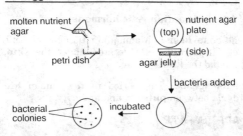

agar Bacteria are cultivated on a nutrient agar plate.

agglutination The process by which **red blood cells** clump together when the **antigens** on their surfaces react with complementary **antibodies**. See **blood groups**, **blood transfusion**.

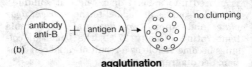

agglutination

agriculture The practice of farming, involving the cultivation of **soil**, crop production and raising livestock.

AIDS (aquired immune deficiency syndrome) A condition caused by a **virus** which weakens the body's immune responses. This results in reduced resistance to diseases such as pneumonia and can be fatal. The virus enters the bloodstream as a result of using contaminated needles, by transfusion of infected blood or bloodproducts, or via sexual contact with an infected person.

alcohol abuse The habitual excessive consumption of alcoholic drinks, which can lead to diseases of the **liver**, **nervous system** and **alimentary canal**.

algae A photosynthetic plant group including **microscopic** types such as *Spirogyra* and *Euglena*, and also **multicellular** types, e.g. seaweeds. Algae are widely distributed as

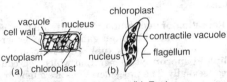

algae   (a) *Spirogyra* (b) *Englena*

marine and freshwater **plankton**, while some seaweeds are edible and others are a source of **agar**.

alimentary canal The digestive canal in animals. In humans it is a tube about nine metres in length running from **mouth** to **anus**. See **digestion**.

alkali A substance which releases hydroxyl ions in water and has a **pH** greater than 7, e.g. *lime* (calcium hydroxide) is added to **soil** to *neutralize* excess **acid**.

alleles Each inherited feature in an individual is produced by a pair of **genes** or alleles, which are located on the **chromosomes**. The pair of genes may produce the same or differing effects. For example, the fruit fly *Drosophila* has a pair of alleles which control wing length. The combination of these dictates the possession of normal wings or vestigial wings. See **monohybrid inheritance, backcross, incomplete dominance**.

alternation of generations The life history of a plant in which a **haploid gametophyte** generation produces by **sexual reproduction** a **diploid sporophyte** generation which reproduces asexually. The two generations are often very different. A similar process is found in some animals such as the jellyfish, in which there are two alternating phases in the life history, but both are diploid.

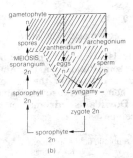

alternation of generations The fern life cycle. n = haploid number of chromosomes.

alveoli Air sacs in the mammalian **lungs** across which **gas exchange** occurs. See **gas exchange (mammals)**.

amino acids **Organic compounds** which are the subunits of **proteins**. Altogether some 70 different amino acids are known, but only about 20–24 are actually found in living organisms, bonded together in chains known as **peptides** which are the basis of protein structure.

R   variable group (depending on amino acid)

$$NH_2 - C - COOH$$

Amino   Acid
group   H   group

amino acid   Structure.

amniocentesis   During   **pregnancy**,   the removal of some fluid from the **amnion**. The fluid contains **cells** from the **foetus**, and by studying their **chromosomes** abnormalities such as **Down's syndrome** or **inherited diseases** can be detected.

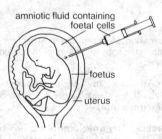

amniotic fluid containing foetal cells

foetus

uterus

amniocentesis

amnion   The fluid-filled sac surrounding and protecting the **embryos** of mammals, birds and reptiles. See **pregnancy**.

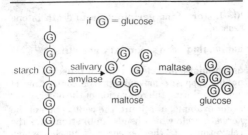

if **G** = glucose

starch →(salivary amylase)→ maltose →(maltase)→ glucose

amylases The action of salivary amylase and maltase.

amylases **Enzymes** which break down **starch** or **glycogen** into **disaccharides** and **glucose** by **hydrolysis**. For example, *salivary amylase*, *maltase*.

anabolism See **metabolism**.

anaerobe An organism which lives in the absence of *oxygen*. See **aerobe**, **respiration**.

androecium The collective name for the male reproductive structures of a **flower**, i.e. the **stamens**.

annual A flowering plant which completes its

life history from **germination** to death in one season.

annual ring   See **secondary growth**.

antagonistic muscles   Pairs of **muscles** which produce opposite movements, the contraction of one stimulating the relaxation of the other.

For example, at a **joint**, the contraction of the *flexor* (muscle which bends limb) stimulates the relaxation of the *extensor* (muscle which straightens limb) so that bending occurs. When the joint straightens due to contraction of the

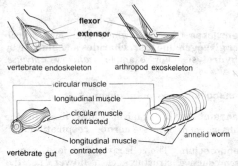

flexor
extensor

vertebrate endoskeleton   arthropod exoskeleton

circular muscle
longitudinal muscle
circular muscle contracted
annelid worm
longitudinal muscle contracted

vertebrate gut

antagonistic muscles   Pairs of muscles pulling in opposite directions perform various functions.

extensor, this causes the flexor to relax.

The longitudinal and circular muscles of the vertebrate **gut** and annelid worms also act antagonistically, the former causing **peristalsis**, and the latter movement.

anterior Describes parts of the body at or near the leading or head end of an animal. Compare **posterior**.

anther In a **flower**, the upper part of a **stamen** containing **pollen** grains.

antibiotics Substances formed by certain **bacteria** and **fungi** which inhibit the growth of other **microorganisms**. For example, **penicillin**, *streptomycin*.

antibiotic discs Sterile paper discs containing **antibiotic**, which are used to identify which antibiotic will be effective against infection with a particular **bacterium**. The discs are added to

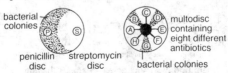

bacterial colonies

penicillin disc

streptomycin disc

multodisc containing eight different antibiotics

bacterial colonies

antibiotic discs Possible results after incubation. Certain antibiotics have destroyed the bacteria.

nutrient agar plates which have been contaminated with bacteria taken from a patient.

In plate A bacteria grow only around the **penicillin** disc, while the plate is clear around the *streptomycin* disc. This shows that not all antibiotics are effective against all **microorganisms**. This is confirmed by plate B in which three of the antibiotics had no effect. See **agar**.

antibiotic resistance The ability of certain **microorganisms** to overcome the action of **antibiotics**: this results from **mutations** producing new strains which are no longer susceptible to the antibiotic.

antibodies **Proteins** produced by vertebrate **tissues** as a reaction to *antigens*, i.e. materials foreign to the organism (for example, **microorganisms** such as bacteria and their **toxins**, or transplanted **organs** or **tissues**). See **agglutination**.

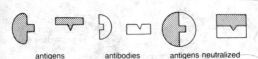

antigens   antibodies   antigens neutralized

antibodies Antibodies react with antigens to make them harmless.

antidiuretic hormone (ADH) A **hormone**

secreted in mammals by the **pituitary gland**, which stimulates water reabsorption by the **kidneys**, thus reducing water loss in the urine.

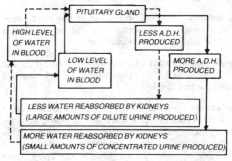

antidiuretic hormone Control of water loss.

antigens See **antibodies**.

antiserum A substance containing large numbers of **antibodies** to a particular **antigen**.

anus The terminal opening of the **alimentary canal** in mammals, through which **faeces** are shed. The anus is opened and closed by a **sphincter muscle**.

aorta The largest **artery** in the **circulatory**

system of mammals; it carries **blood** from the left **ventricle** of the **heart** to the rest of the body.

apical growth See **primary growth**.

appendix A small sac found at the junction of the **ileum** and **caecum** of some mammals. In humans its function is unclear.

aqueous humour Clear watery fluid filling the front chamber of the vertebrate **eye** between the **cornea** and the **lens**.

arteries Vessels which transport **blood** from the **heart** to the **tissues**. In mammals, arteries carry *oxygenated* blood (for an exception to this rule, see **pulmonary vessels**) and divide into smaller vessels called *arterioles*. They have thick, elastic, muscular walls, in order to withstand the high pressure caused by the heartbeat.

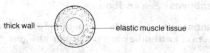

thick wall —— —— elastic muscle tissue

artery Section through an artery.

artificial propagation The method by which plant growers make use of a plant's capacity for **asexual reproduction** and **regeneration** in order to produce new plants. Small pieces of

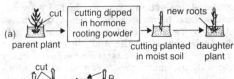

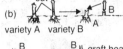

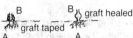

artificial propagation (a) Cutting (b) grafting (c) layering.

stems, roots or leaves are taken and under the right conditions these will grow into new plants (**clones**). Three methods are shown here.

artificial selection The method by which animal and plant breeders attempt to improve stocks by selecting the males and females with desirable characteristics and allowing them to interbreed. By rigorous selection over many generations, improvements can be made in stock quality, e.g. in beef and milk production in cattle or yield and disease resistance in crops. See **natural selection**.

asexual reproduction **Reproduction** in which new organisms are formed from a single parent without **gamete** production. The offspring from asexual reproduction are genetically identical to each other and to the parent organism, and are referred to as a **clone**. See **binary fission**, **budding**, **spore**, **vegetative reproduction**.

assimilation (of food) The process by which digested food particles are incorporated into the **protoplasm** of an organism. For example, in mammals glucose not required immediately to provide energy in tissue respiration is converted in **liver** and **muscle cells** to the storage **carbohydrate glycogen** which can be reconverted to glucose if the blood glucose level falls. (See **insulin**.) Excess glucose not stored as glycogen is converted to **fat** and stored in fat storage cells beneath the **skin**, as a long term energy store.

Fatty acids and *glycerol* are reassembled into

fat. Excess fat is stored as outlined above.

Amino acids are synthesized into **proteins**. Excess amino acids cannot be stored and are disposed of in the liver by **deamination**.

atom The smallest complete particle of an **element** that can exist chemically. Each atom consists of a nucleus of **protons** and **neutrons** surrounded by moving **electrons**. See **molecule**.

ATP (adenosine triphosphate) A chemical compound which acts as a store and a source of **energy** within **cells**. ATP is formed from *adenosine diphosphate* (ADP) and a *phosphate group* using energy from **respiration** which can then be released for metabolic processes when ATP is broken down.

ATP ATP provides energy for metabolic processes.

atrium or **auricle** See **heart, heartbeat**.

auditory Describes part of the body and functions related to the **ear**.

auditory canal A tube in the mammalian outer **ear** leading from the **pinna** to the **tympanum**.

✓**auditory nerve**   A *cranial nerve* in vertebrates conducting **nerve impulses** from the *inner ear* to the **brain**. See **ear**.

auricle or **atrium**   See **heart**, **heartbeat**.

autoclave   A pressure cooker used for the **sterilization** of materials e.g. **agar** before and after use in **microbiology** experiments. The materials to be sterilised are heated in the autoclave at 120°C for 15 minutes to destroy any **bacteria** present.

autoradiograph   A picture obtained when a photographic negative is exposed to living **tissue** into which *radioactive* material has been introduced in order to trace the route of substances through the tissue.

autotrophic or **holophytic**   Describing organisms which synthesize complex **organic compounds** from simple non-living **inorganic compounds**. The major autotrophs are green plants which use water and carbon dioxide to make food by **photosynthesis**. For this reason green plants are also called **food producers**. Compare **heterotrophic**.

auxins   Plant **hormones** which control many aspects of plant growth, for example, **tropisms**, by stimulating **cell division** and elongation.

axon See **neurones**, **synapse**.

backbone See **vertebral column**.

backcross A **genetic** cross in which a **heterozygous** organism is crossed with one of its **homozygous** parents. Thus two backcrosses are possible.

For example, in the fruit fly *Drosophila*, normal wings are **dominant** to vestigial wings and

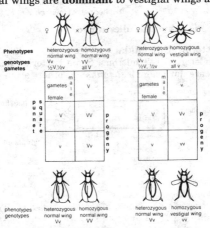

backcross The two backcrosses of *Drosophila*.

so heterozygous flies will have normal wings. The backcross with the **recessive** homozygote is useful in distinguishing between organisms with the same **phenotype** but different **genotypes**. For example, *VV.* and *Vv.* Such a cross is called a **testcross**:

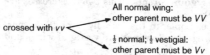

crossed with *vv* → All normal wing: other parent must be *VV*

→ ½ normal; ½ vestigial: other parent must be *Vv*

See **monohybrid inheritance**.

bacteria Unicellular organisms with a diameter of 1–2 microns. Some bacteria cause disease, for example, *tetanus* but others are use-

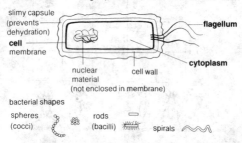

slimy capsule (prevents dehydration)

flagellum

cell membrane

nuclear material (not enclosed in membrane)

cell wall

cytoplasm

bacterial shapes

spheres (cocci)

rods (bacilli)

spirals

bacteria Structure of a generalized bacterium, with bacterial shapes.

ful, for example, as sources of **antibiotics**.

Baermann funnel An apparatus used to isolate organisms living in soil water, e.g. **algae**, **protozoa**. The organisms move away from the strong light and high temperature of the lamp and collect near the tap, from where they can be released into the collecting jar.

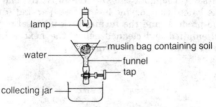

Baermann funnel

balanced diet The correct nutritional components required for health, generally used in reference to human beings and domesticated animals. A balanced diet for humans should contain:

(a) Sufficient kilojoules of **energy**;
(b) **Protein**;
(c) **Carbohydrate**;
(d) **Fat**;
(e) **Vitamins**;
(f) **Water**;
(g) **Mineral salts**;
(h) **Roughage**.

basal metabolic rate (BMR) The rate of **metabolism** of a resting animal as measured by oxygen consumption. BMR is the minimum amount of **energy** needed to maintain life and varies with **species**, age and sex.

batch processing In **biotechnology**, an industrial process in which the **enzymes** are dispersed throughout the **substrate**. At the end of the batch, the enzyme has to be separated from the product, and the **fermentation** vessel must be emptied and cleaned before the next batch. See **continuous flow processing**.

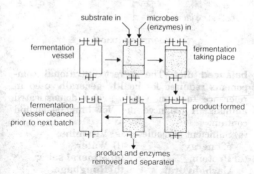

batch processing

bile A green alkaline fluid produced in the **liver** of mammals. Bile is stored in the **gall bladder** and is transported via the *bile duct* to the **duodenum** where it causes **fat** to be broken into minute droplets (emulsification) before digestion. See **digestion**.

binary fission **Asexual reproduction** in **unicellular** organisms in which a single **cell** divides to produce two cells. The nucleus divides by **mitosis**. Binary fission is common in **bacteria** and **protozoa** such as *Amoeba* where a single mother cell divides into two identical daughter cells.

binary fission *Amoeba.*

binomial nomenclature The method of naming organisms devised by Carl Von Linne (Linnaeus) in the 18th century. Each organism has two Latin names, the first, with an initial capital, indicating the **genus**, and the second with a lower case first letter indicating **species**. (See **classification**.) For example:

Genus	Species	Common name
Canis	*familiaris*	domestic dog
Canis	*lupus*	American wolf

biodegradable Able to be readily broken down by biological action. For example, detergents in **sewage** can be digested by **bacteria**.

biological clock The mechanism thought to be responsible for animal **rhythmical behaviour** patterns associated with repeating natural cycles such as tides, **photoperiods** and seasons.

biological control The use of natural **predators**, **pathogens** and **parasites** to control **pests**.

biological detergents Powders containing **enzymes** obtained from **bacteria**. These enzymes break down stains caused by **proteins** in milk, **blood**, egg etc. The stains are converted by the enzymes into soluble substances which can be washed away.

biomass The total mass of living matter in a **population**. Biomass is usually expressed as living or dry weight and decreases at each level in a **food chain**. See **pyramid of numbers**, **pyramid of biomass**.

biosphere That part of the Earth which contains living organisms. The biosphere includes all the various **habitats** from the deepest oceans to the highest mountains. See **environment**.

biotechnology The use of living organisms in manufacturing processes. For example, **microorganisms** are used in ethanol production by **fermentation**, **brewing** with **yeast**, and **enzyme** production.

biotic factor See **environment**.

birth (in humans) The human baby is born as a result of muscular contractions of the **uterus** wall. The *amniotic fluid*, in which the baby has been floating, escapes, and the baby is pushed through the **cervix** and the **vagina** and thus leaves the mother's body.

The **umbilical cord** is cut, the **placenta** is expelled as the *afterbirth* and the baby must now use its own **lungs** for **gas exchange**. See **fertilization**, **pregnancy**.

birth rate Of a **population**, the number of live births, measured in the human population as number of births in one year per 1000 of population. See **human population curve**.

bladder (urinary) A sac into which **urine** from the **kidneys** passes via the **ureters**. From the bladder, urine is discharged through the **urethra**. See **kidney**.

blind spot The blind spot in the **eye** can be demonstrated by a simple experiment, as follows.

Hold the book at arm's length. Close the left eye and concentrate on the cross with the right eye. Slowly bring the book closer until the drawing of the face seems to disappear. At this point the image of the face is falling on the blind spot.

blind spot

blood A fluid **tissue** found in many animals with the principal function of transporting substances from one part of the body to another. In mammals, blood consists of a watery solution called **plasma**, in which there are three types of cells: **platelets**, **red blood cells** and **white blood cells**.

The main functions of blood are:

(a) Transport of *oxygen* from **lungs** to **tissues**;

(b) Transport of toxic by-products to the **organs** of **excretion**;

(c) Transport of **hormones** from **endocrine glands** to target organs;

(d) Transport of digested food from the **ileum** to the tissue;

(e) Prevention of infection by **blood clotting**, **phagocytosis** by white blood cells, and **antibody** production.

blood clotting The conversion of **blood plasma** into a clot, which occurs when blood **platelets** are exposed to air as a result of injury. The platelets produce an **enzyme** (*thrombin*) which causes the conversion of a soluble **plasma protein** (**fibrinogen**) into *fibrin*, which forms a meshwork of fibres and the resulting clot restricts blood loss and the entry of **microorganisms**.

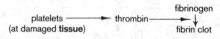

blood clotting The process of clot formation.

blood groups The classification of **blood** types based on the different **antigens** present on the surface of **red blood cells**.

The human **population** is divided into four groups called A, B, AB and O. The capital letters stand for the type of antigen present in the red blood cells. The corresponding **antibodies** are carried in the **plasma**, and if a person has a particular antigen in his red cells, he cannot have the corresponding antibody since **agglutination** would occur. Thus

Group A contains antigen A and antibody anti-B.
Group B contains antigen B and antibody anti-A.
Group AB contains antigens A and B and no

antibodies of either type.

Group O has no antigens and antibodies anti-A and anti-B.

See **blood transfusion**.

blood group	antigen on red blood cells	antibody in plasma
A	A	anti-B
B	B	anti-A
AB	A and B	neither
O	neither	anti-A and anti-B

blood groups

blood pressure The pressure of **blood** in the main **arteries** of mammals. In humans, blood pressure is normally between about 120 mm mercury (Hg) at **systole** and about 80 mm Hg at **diastole**, but can vary with age, **exercise** etc. See **heartbeat**.

blood serum Fluid consisting of **blood plasma** with the **fibrinogen** removed.

blood tests The use of **agglutination** in order to determine a person's **blood group**. If one drop of blood from a sample is mixed with *Anti-A* **blood serum** and another drop with *anti-B* blood serum then:

Group A **red blood cells** will clump only in
anti-A;

Group B **red blood cells** will clump only in
anti-B;

Group AB **red blood cells** will clump in both
antisera;

Group O **red blood cells** will clump in neither
antiserum.

See **agglutination, blood groups, blood
transfusions**.

blood group under test	antigens on cells	antibodies in plasma	added to anti-A test serum	added to anti-B test serum
A	A	anti-B	clumped	scattered
B	B	anti-A	scattered	clumped
AB	A and B	neither	clumped	clumped
O	neither	anti-A anti-B	scattered	scattered

blood tests Summary.

blood transfusion The transfer of **blood** from
a healthy person (the *donor*) to another person

who has lost a lot of blood, e.g. as a result of an injury. The **blood groups** of the donor and the patient must match or else the **antibodies** in the patient's **plasma** will act upon the **antigens** on the donor's **red blood cells** and cause the cells to clump together (**agglutination**).
See **blood groups**.

blood group	can donate blood to:	can receive blood from:
A	A and AB	A and O
B	B and AB	B and O
AB	AB	all groups
O	all groups	O

blood transfusion Table showing the pattern of blood acceptability.

blood vessels Tubes transporting **blood** around the bodies of many animals, which together with the **heart** make up the **circulatory system**. In vertebrates, the blood vessels consist of **arteries**, *arterioles*, **capillaries**, *venules*, and **veins**.

BMR See **basal metabolic rate**.

bone Tissue in the vertebrate **skeleton** consisting of **collagen** (a **protein**) which gives *ten-*

sile strength, and calcium phosphate which gives bone its hardness. Some bones have a hollow cavity containing bone marrow in which new **red blood cells** are produced.

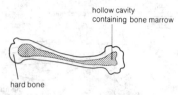

hollow cavity
containing bone marrow

hard bone

bone Section through bone.

Bowman's capsule In mammals, a cup-shaped part of a **kidney** tubule or **nephron**.

brain The large mass of **nerve cells** in animals which has a centralized coordinating function. In vertebrates it is found at the **anterior** end of the body, protected by the **cranium**, and connected to the body, via the **spinal cord** and its *spinal nerves*, or directly by nerves called *cranial nerves*, e.g. **optic nerve**, **auditory nerve**.

The human brain contains millions of nerve cells which are continually receiving and sending out **nerve impulses**. The remarkable property of the brain is that it translates electrical impulses in such a way that stimuli from the **environment**, such as sound and light, are

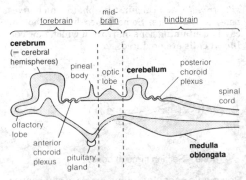

brain Diagram of the vertebrate brain.

appreciated so that the recipient of the stimuli can respond and adapt to the environment in the most appropriate way. The brain also coordinates bodily activities to ensure efficient operation, and stores information so that behaviour can be modified as the result of experience.

breastbone See **sternum**.

breathing (in mammals) The inhalation and exhalation of air for the purpose of **gas exchange**. In mammals the gas exchange surface is situated in the **lungs**.

The exchange of air in the lungs (*ventilation*) is

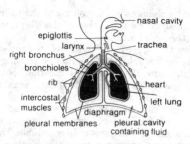

Breathing Lungs and associated structures.

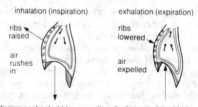

breathing Movements of the rib cage.

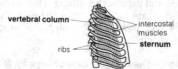

caused by changes in the volume of the **thorax**, brought about by the action of the **diaphragm** and **intercostal muscles**.

When the diaphragm contracts, it depresses, increasing the volume of the thorax, causing air to rush into the lungs. Relaxation of the diaphragm reduces the volume of the thorax, and causes exhalation of air. The action of the diaphragm is accompanied by the raising and lowering of the rib cage, which is necessary to accommodate the changes in lung volume. These rib cage movements are caused by contraction and relaxation of the intercostal muscles.

breathing rate The rate of **lung** ventilation. In humans, **breathing** movements are controlled by the **medulla oblongata** in the **brain**, which is sensitive to the *carbon dioxide* concentration of the **blood**. If the carbon dioxide concentration rises sharply as the result of increased **respiration**, for example, during exercise, the brain sends **nerve impulses** to the **diaphragm** and **intercostal muscles** which react by increasing the rate and depth of breathing. This accelerated breathing rate helps to expel the excess carbon dioxide and increases the supply of oxygen to respiring cells.

brewing The manufacture of beer by **fermentation**. The main stages are as follows.

1) Germinating barley grains convert

$$starch \xrightarrow{\textbf{enzymes}} sugar \ (\textit{malting})$$

2) sugar+**yeast**+hops

|

fermentation

↓

alcohol+carbon dioxide
(beer)

Other alcoholic brews can be manufactured using **substrates** other than barley and hops, e.g. apple juice (to make cider), grape juice (wine), rice (sake) and honey (mead).

bronchus One of two air passages branching from the **trachea** in lunged vertebrates. See **lungs**.

budding **Asexual reproduction** in which a new organism develops as an outgrowth or *bud* from the parent, the offspring often becoming completely detached from the parent. Budding is common among coelenterates, e.g. *Hydra* and **unicellular fungi,** e.g. **yeast**. See diagram on page 38.

buffer A **solution** which maintains a constant **pH** even on the addition of an **acid** or an **alkali**.

bulb The **organ** of **vegetative reproduction**

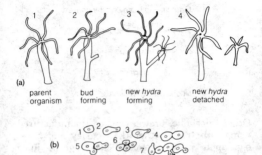

(a)
parent organism — bud forming — new *hydra* forming — new *hydra* detached

(b)

budding (a) *Hydra* (b) yeast.

in flowering plants, consisting of a modified **shoot** whose short **stem** is enclosed by fleshy scale-like **leaves**. In the growing season, one or more buds within the bulb develop into new plants, using food stored in the bulb.

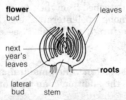

bulb Section through bulb.

Bulb-producing plants include the *tulip*, *daffodil* and *onion*.

caecum Part of the mammalian **gut** at the entry to the large **intestine**. In **herbivores** it is very important in **cellulose digestion**. In humans it is much reduced in size and its function is uncertain.

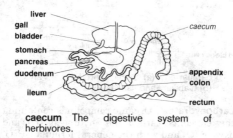

caecum The digestive system of herbivores.

cambium Plant **meristem** within **vascular bundle** which forms new **xylem** and **phloem** cells during **secondary growth**.

canines Sharp-pointed tearing **teeth** near the front of the mouth used for killing prey, and ripping off pieces of food. Often reduced or missing in **herbivores**, present in **omnivores** and prominent in **carnivores**. See **dental formula**, **dentition**.

capillaries   **Blood vessels** formed from *arterioles* and forming a network in vertebrate **tissues**, the **blood** eventually draining into *venules* and then **veins**.

Capillary walls are only one **cell** thick, allowing **diffusion** of substances between the blood and the tissues via a liquid called *tissue fluid* (**lymph**).

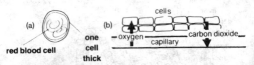

capillaries   (a) Section through capillary. (b) Capillary and tissues.

carbohydrates   Organic compounds containing the elements carbon (C), hydrogen (H) and oxygen (O) and with the general formula CH_2O. Carbohydrates are either individual **sugar** units or chains of sugar units bonded together.

Importance of carbohydrates:
(a) Simple carbohydrates, particularly **glucose**, are the principal **energy** source within cells;
(b) Long-chain carbohydrates form some structural cell components, for example, **cellulose**, in plant cell walls, and also act as food reserves, for example, **glycogen** in animals and **starch** in plants.

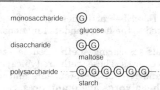

carbohydrates The three main carbohydrate types are **monosaccharides**, **disaccharides**, and **polysaccharides**.

carbon cycle The circulation of the **element
carbon** and its compounds, in nature, caused
mainly by the **metabolism** of living organisms.

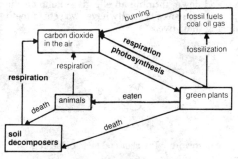

carbon cycle The main steps.

cardiac Describes activities and parts of the body related to the **heart** and its functions.

carnassials Shearing **teeth** used for cutting meat into chunks. These teeth are typical of **carnivores** and replace the premolars and molars found in **herbivores** and **omnivores**. See **dental formula**, **dentition**.

carnivore An animal that feeds on flesh. Carnivores include dogs, cats, etc. They have a **dentition** adapted for killing prey, shearing raw flesh, and cracking bones. The outstanding features of carnivore dentition are the large piercing **canine teeth**, and the shearing **carnassial** teeth. The lower jaw can usually only move up and down, forming an effective clamp on the prey. Carnivores typically have two sets of teeth during their lives.

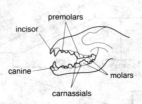

carnivore The skull and teeth of the dog.

carpel The female part of a **flower** containing

an **ovary** in which there are varying numbers of **ovules** containing **embryo sacs**, within which are the female **gametes**.
See **fertilization**.

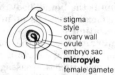

stigma
style
ovary wall
ovule
embryo sac
micropyle
female gamete

carpel The female reproductive part of a flower.

cartilage Supporting **tissue** found in vertebrates. In mammals there is cartilage in the **larynx**, **trachea**, **bronchi** and at the ends of **bones** at moveable **joints**, while in some fish, e.g. sharks, the entire skeleton is cartilage.

catabolism See **metabolism**.

catalyst A substance which accelerates a chemical reaction but does not become part of the end product. See **enzyme**.

caudal Describes that part of the body of an animal at or near the tail.

cell A unit of **cytoplasm** governed by a single **nucleus** and surrounded by a **selectively permeable membrane**. Cells are the basic units of which most living things are made.

The **nucleus** contains the hereditary material, the **chromosomes**, and controls the cell's activities.

The **cytoplasm** is the liquid 'body' of the cell in which the chemical reactions of life occur, for example, **respiration**.

The **cell membrane** controls the entry and exit of materials, allowing certain substances through, but preventing the passage of others. Such a membrane is described as a selectively permeable membrane.

The **cell wall** is found only in plants. It is made of **cellulose** and gives shape and rigidity to the cells.

The **chloroplasts** are structures within green plant cells where **photosynthesis** occurs.

The **vacuole** is filled with cell sap in plants. The sap, when in sufficient quantity, creates a pressure on the cytoplasm and cell wall and helps keep the cell firm and resilient. See **Protoplasm**.

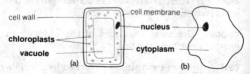

cell Structure of (a) a plant cell and (b) an animal cell.

cell differentiation The process of change in **cells** during **growth** and development, whereby previously *undifferentiated* cells become specialized for a particular function as a result of structural changes.

For example in plant cells, after **cell division**, the *daughter cells* increase in size (elongation), by absorbing water.

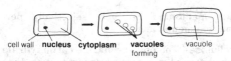

cell wall   nucleus   cytoplasm   vacuoles   vacuole
                                     forming

    cell differentiation Elongation in plant cells.

After elongation, cell differentiation occurs as the result of **protoplasm** and *cell wall* changes. For example:

(a) Some cells have their walls strengthened by additional **cellulose**, e.g. **cortex**, **epidermis**.

(b) Some cells have **lignin** deposited in their walls, e.g. **xylem**.

(c) Some cells develop extra *organelles*, for example, the high number of **chloroplasts** in the **palisade mesophyll** cells of leaves.

cell division The division of the **cell** and its contents into two. The nucleus usually divides by

mitosis, a process which gives the **nuclei** of the *daughter cells* exactly the same number of **chromosomes** as the *mother nucleus*. When a cell divides to form **gametes** (sex cells) the nucleus divides by **meiosis** which provides *daughter nuclei* with half the original number of chromosomes. In animals the **cytoplasm** divides by constriction into two. In plants a wall is laid down between the two halves.

cell membrane See **cell, selectively permeable membrane**.

cellulose The **polysaccharide carbohydrate** which forms the framework and gives strength to plant **cell** walls. Cellulose remains undigested in the human **gut** but has an important role as **roughage**. In mammalian **herbivores**, in the **caecum** and **appendix**, **bacterial populations** produce an **enzyme** called *cellulase* which digests cellulose. See **digestion**.

cellulose The breakdown of cellulose into glucose by the action of cellulase.

cell wall See **cell**.

central nervous system (CNS)   That part of the vertebrate **nervous system** which has the highest concentration of **nerve cell** bodies and **synapses**, i.e. the **brain** and **spinal cord**.

cerebellum   The region of the vertebrate **brain** which in mammals controls balance and muscular coordination, allowing precise controlled movements in activities such as walking and running.

cerebrum (cerebral hemispheres)   The region of vertebrate **brain** which in mammals makes up the largest part of the brain. In humans the cerebrum consists of right and left hemispheres, the outer part made up of **neurone cell bodies** (*grey matter*), the inner part consists of **nerve fibres** (*white matter*). The human cerebrum is responsible for the higher mental skills such as memory, thought, reasoning and intelligence. The cerebrum also contains localized areas concerned with specific functions. Areas receiving

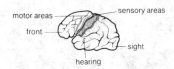

cerebrum   Left cerebral hemisphere of human, showing localization of functions.

nerve impulses from **receptors** are called *sensory areas*, while those sending out impulses to **effectors** are called *motor areas*.

cervical Describes parts of the body and functions related to (a) the neck, (b) the **cervix**.

cervix The posterior region of mammalian **uterus**, leading into the **vagina**. See **fertilization**.

chemoreceptor A **receptor** which is stimulated by chemical substances, e.g. **smell** and **taste** receptors.

chemotropism **Tropism** relative to chemical substances. The growth of **pollen** tubes towards the **ovary** is an example of positive chemotropism. See **fertilization**.

chlorophyll Green pigment found in the **chloroplasts** of plant cells which can absorb the light **energy** required for **photosynthesis**. The

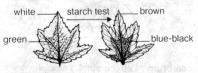

white — starch test — brown
green — blue-black

chlorophyll The variegated leaf test.

importance of chlorophyll can be shown by testing a variegated leaf for **starch**. Only those parts which were previously green give a positive starch test, showing that chlorophyll is necessary for photosynthesis.

chloroplasts Structures in the **cytoplasm** of green plant **cells**, in which **photosynthesis** occurs. Chloroplasts contain the green pigment **chlorophyll**.

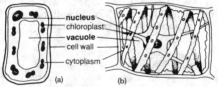

nucleus
chloroplast
vacuole
cell wall
cytoplasm

(a)   (b)

chloroplasts The chloroplasts of (a) a palisade mesophyll cell and (b) the alga *Spirogyra*.

choroid Layer of **cells** outside the **retina** of the vertebrate **eye**.

chromosomes The hereditary material within the **nucleus** of **cells**, which links one generation with the next. Each **species** has characteristic numbers and types of chromosomes.

For example, in humans, the chromosome number is 46. When a nucleus divides by **mitosis** this **diploid** number of chromosomes is maintained in the new nuclei formed. **Haploid** nuclei contain half the diploid number of chromosomes, and are made when the nucleus divides by **meiosis**. Two haploid **gametes** join to form a diploid **zygote**.

Chromosomes control cellular activity. They consist of sub-units called **genes** which contain coded information in the form of the chemical compound **DNA**. In diploid cells, chromosomes occur in similar pairs known as homologous pairs. Thus a human diploid cell contains 23 pairs of **homologous chromosomes**.

chromatid ——
centromere ——

homologous
chromosomes

chromosomes A pair of homologous chromosomes.

cilia Microscopic motile threads projecting from certain **cell** surfaces which stroke rhythmically together like oars. Cilia occur in certain vertebrate **epithelia** where they cause movement of particles in the **trachea**, **oviduct**, **uterus**, etc. In some **protozoa** e.g. *Paramecium*, cilia cause movement of the whole organism. Compare **flagellum**.

cilia The cilia of (a) epithelial cells and (b) *Paramecium*.

ciliary muscle Tissue in the vertebrate **eye** responsible for **accommodation**.

circulatory system Any system of vessels in animals through which fluids circulate, e.g. the **blood** circulation, **lymphatic system**.

In mammals there are two overlapping blood circulations, i.e., there is a circulation between **heart** and **lungs** and a circulation between heart and body. This arrangement is called a double circulatory system. Blood flows through both circulations, always in the same direction, passing repeatedly through the heart. See diagram on page 52.

class A unit used in the **classification** of living organisms, consisting of one or more **orders**.

classification The method of arranging living

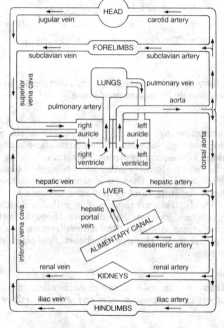

circulatory system The double circulatory system of mammals.

organisms on the basis of similarity of structure into groups which show how closely they are related to each other and also indicate evolutionary relationships. The modern system of classification was devised by Carl von Linne (Linnaeus) in the eighteenth century. Organisms are first sorted into large groups called **kingdoms** which are divided into smaller groups called **phyla** in animals and **divisions** in plants, then **classes**, **orders** and **families**, each subdivision producing subsets containing fewer and fewer organisms, but with more and more common features. Ultimately organisms are grouped in genera (singular **genus**) which are groups of closely related **species**. It is not uncommon for scientists to disagree as to how to classify certain organisms. See table on page 54.

clavicle or **collarbone**. The ventral **bone** of the shoulder-girdle of many vertebrates articulating with the **scapula** and **sternum**. See **endo-skeleton**.

cloaca The posterior region of the **alimentary canal** in most vertebrates (but excluding mammals) into which the terminal part of the **intestine** and the **kidney** and reproductive ducts open.

clone A group of organisms which are geneti-

	Human	Dog	Oak	Meadow buttercup
Kingdom	Animal	Animal	Plant	Plant
Phylum/Order	Chordata	Chordata	Spermatophyta	Spermatophyta
Class	Mammalia	Mammalia	Angiospermae	Angiospermae
Order	Primates	Carnivora	Fagales	Ranales
Family	Hominidae	Canidae	Fagaceae	Ranunculaceae
Genus	*Homo*	*Canis*	*Quercus*	*Ranunculus*
Species	*sapiens*	*familiaris*	*robur*	*acris*

classification How four organisms are classified.

cally identical to each other, having been produced by **asexual reproduction**.

cloning methods   See **artificial propagation**.

cochlea   A spiral structure in the mammalian inner **ear** containing an area called the *organ of corti* in which are located **nerve cell** endings which are sensitive to sound vibrations.

codominance   A situation in which both **alleles** are expressed equally in the **phenotype** of a **heterozygote**.

The inheritance of human **blood groups** includes an example of codominance. There are four blood group phenotypes. A, B, AB and O. The **genes** for groups A and B are codominant

phenotype (blood group)	genotype
A	I^AI^A or I^AI^O
B	I^BI^B or I^BI^O
AB	I^AI^B
O	I^OI^O

co-dominance   The phenotypes and **genotypes** of the four blood groups using the symbol I to represent the alleles.

and both are completely dominant to the gene for group O. Thus if a person inherits genes for group A and group B, half his **red blood cells** will carry **antigen** A and half antigen B.

CNS See **central nervous system**.

cold-blooded See **poikilothermic**.

collagen Fibrous **protein**, which is the principal component of vertebrate **connective tissue**, and an important skeletal substance in higher animals, conferring tensile strength to **bones**, **tendons**, and **ligaments**.

collarbone See **clavicle**.

colon A region of the **large intestine** in mammals between the **caecum** and **rectum**, which receives undigested food from the **ileum**. In the colon, much of the water is absorbed from the undigested food, and the semi-solid remains (**faeces**) are passed into the **rectum**. See **digestion**.

commensalism A symbiotic relationship in which one of the organisms benefits, while the other neither suffers nor benefits. For example, a marine worm lives in a shell with a crab, sharing the crab's food, but giving nothing in return. See **symbiosis**.

community The **population** of different **species** living in a particular **habitat** and interacting with each other. For example, a rockpool habitat may have a community made up of crabs, worms, sponges, seaweeds, etc. See **niche**.

companion cell In flowering plants, companion cells are associated with **phloem sieve tubes**, and are believed to contribute to the transport function of phloem (**translocation**).

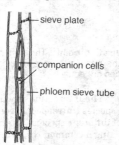

sieve plate

companion cells

phloem sieve tube

companion cell

compensation point *(of green plants)* The light intensity at which the rate of carbon dioxide uptake (**photosynthesis**) is exactly equal to the rate of carbon dioxide production (**respiration**). In a single day there are two compensation points when the rate of photosynthesis (**carbo-**

hydrate gain) is exactly balanced by the rate of respiration (carbohydrate loss).

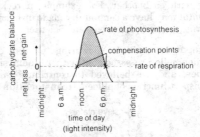

compensation point The two points at which the rates of photosynthesis and of respiration are equal.

competition The interaction among organisms of the same species (intraspecific competition) or organisms of different species (interspecific competition) seeking a common resource such as food or light which is in limited supply in the area occupied by the **community**. Competition often

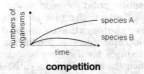

competition

results in the elimination of one organism by another, or even in the elimination of one species as happens when two species of *paramecium* compete for food.

compound A chemical formed by the combination of **elements** with the component **atoms** occurring in fixed proportions. The basic unit of a compound is the **molecule** whose formation requires a chemical reaction. Mixtures, unlike compounds, have variable proportions of component atoms and can be separated by physical means.

conception An alternative term for **fertilization**.

conditioned reflex A **response** to a **stimulus** that has been learned by an animal as a result of the repeated association of the stimulus, which may be neutral, to a particular effect that is related to the learned response. For example, a rat may learn to press a lever when hungry as a result of learning to associate the lever's movement with the delivery of food. See **sensitivity**.

cone 1. A reproductive structure of gymnosperms, e.g. pines.
2. Light-sensitive **nerve cell** in the **retina** of most vertebrate **eyes**. Sensitive in bright light, they can detect colour.

connective tissue Supporting and packing **tissue** in vertebrates, consisting mainly of **collagen** fibres, in which are embedded more complex structures, such as **blood vessels**, **nerve fibres**, etc.

continuous flow processing In **biotechnology**, an industrial process in which the **substrates** flow continuously into the **fermentation** vessel and the product flows out continuously. This is made possible by using immobilized **enzymes** which can be used over and over again.

Continuous flow processing is more efficient than **batch processing** since the enzymes can be used repeatedly, the product does not have to be separated from the enzymes, and no time-consuming turn-around is involved.

See **batch processing, immobilization**.

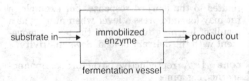

substrate in → immobilized enzyme → product out

fermentation vessel

continuous flow processing

continous variation See **variation**.

contractile vacuole A small sac in the **cytoplasm** of freshwater Protista, the function of which is **osmoregulation**, i.e., in response to water entry by **osmosis**, the vacuole expands as it fills with water, and then contracts, discharging its contents out of the **cell**.

(a) contractile vacuoles (b) contractile vacuole

contractile vacuole The contractile vacuoles of (a) *Paramecium* and (b) *Amoeba*.

control experiment A test set up in a scientific investigation in which the factor being investigated is kept constant, so that the result of another test in which this factor is varied can be compared. See **scientific method**.

copulation The coupling of male and female animals for the purpose of **fertilization**. In humans the **penis** is inserted in the **vagina** and the **spermatazoa** are released.

corm An **organ** of **vegetative reproduction** in flowering plants consisting of an underground **stem** containing a food store and buds which develop into new plants. Examples of corms include those of the crocus and gladiolus.

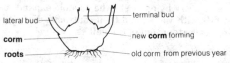

lateral bud — | — terminal bud
corm | — new **corm** forming
roots | — old corm from previous year

corm   Section through a crocus corm.

cornea   Transparent **tissue** at the front surface of the vertebrate **eye**, continuous with the **sclerotic** and involved in focusing the image on the **retina**.

cortex   1. *Animals*: The outer layer of an organ, for example, mammalian **kidney**. See **medulla**. 2. *Plants*: Layer of **cells** between the **epidermis** and the **vascular bundles**. Cortex cells are packing and supporting tissue, and in some cases, may store food. See **leaf**, **root**, **stem**.

cotyledon   An embryonic **leaf** within a **seed** which supplies food during **germination**, and in some plants is brought above the soil to carry out **photosynthesis** for a time before withering. Flowering plants with one cotyledon are called **monocotyledons**, and those with two are called **dicotyledons**.

courtship behaviour   A   type   of   animal

behaviour which establishes contact between the sexes and thus increases the chance of successful breeding, e.g. bird song and display.

cranial Describes activities and parts of the body related to the **brain** and **cranium**.

cranium The **bones** of the vertebrate skull which enclose and protect the **brain**. See **endoskeleton**.

crop rotation The practice of growing a different crop in the same area in successive years in order to prevent **soil depletion**. Since different plants have different **mineral salt** requirements, changing the crop annually prevents depletion of one particular mineral salt. Another benefit is that since different plants have different **root** lengths, they absorb mineral salts from different **soil** depths. Leguminous plants are often included in rotations because of the **nitrogen fixation** within their **root nodules**. A typical crop rotation might be wheat/turnips/barley/clover/wheat, etc.

crossing over See **meiosis**.

cuticle A noncellular layer secreted by the **epidermis** of plant aerial structures and by many invertebrates. Plant cuticles reduce water loss by **transpiration**, while invertebrate cuticles afford protection against mechanical damage and may also retain or repel water.

cytoplasm That part of the **protoplasm** of a cell bounded by the **cell membrane** but excluding the **nucleus.**

deamination Removal of the *amino* ($-NH_2$) group from excess **amino acids**. In mammals, this occurs in the **liver**, the amino group automatically changing to the toxic compound *ammonia* (NH_3) which is then converted to **urea** and excreted. The remaining carbon-containing group is converted to useful **carbohydrate**.

deamination The results of deamination in mammalian liver.

death rate Of a **population**, the number of deaths, measured in the human population as the number of deaths in one year per 1000 of population. See **human population curve**.

decay The process by which **decomposers** use

the organic matter of dead organisms as a source of energy. See **carbon cycle**, **nitrogen cycle**.

decomposers Heterotrophic organisms which cause the breakdown of dead animals and plants, and by so doing release their constituent compounds which can be used by other organisms. **Soil** decomposers include **bacteria**, earthworms, etc. See **carbon cycle, nitrogen cycle**.

denaturation Changes occurring in the structure and functioning of **proteins** (including **enzymes**) when subjected to extremes of temperature or **pH**.

dendrite or **dendron** See **neurones, synapse**.

denitrification The conversion by **soil** *denitrifying bacteria* of *nitrates* into nitrogen which can re-enter the atmosphere. See **nitrogen cycle**.

dental formula A formula describing the **dentition** of a mammal and expressed by writing the number of **teeth** in the upper jaw of one side of the mouth over the number of teeth in the lower jaw on one side. See diagram on page 66. Dental formula refers to an adult mammal with the correct number of teeth. The total number of teeth is found by doubling the dental formula. See **car-**

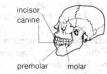

dental formula – incisor ²⁄₂ canine¹⁄₁ premolar ²⁄₂ molar ³⁄₃

total number of teeth = 2 × dental formula
= 2 × 16 = 32

dental formula Diagram illustrating the human dental formula.

nivore, **herbivore**.

dentition The numbers and types of **teeth** in a mammal, described by a **dental formula**. Dentition reflects an animal's diet, i.e., an animal has the type of teeth best suited to deal with the type of food on which it feeds. See **carnivore, herbivore, omnivore**.

deoxyribonucleic acid See **DNA**.

diaphragm A dome-shaped **muscle** separating the **thorax** and **abdomen** in mammals. Contraction and relaxation of the diaphragm is important in **lung** ventilation. See **breathing**.

diastema A toothless gap in the mouth of many **herbivores**, allowing the tongue to manipulate food more easily.

diastole See **heartbeat**.

dicotyledons One of the two subsets of flowering plants, the other being **monocotyledons**. The characteristics of dicotyledons are:

(a) Two cotyledons in the **seed**;
(b) Network of branching **veins** in **leaves**;
(c) Broad leaves;
(d) Ring of **vascular bundles** in **stem**;
(e) Flower parts in fours or fives or multiples of these numbers.

Examples: hardwood trees, fruit trees, herbaceous plants. See **secondary growth**.

diffusion The movement of particles from a region of high concentration to a region of lower concentration until they are evenly distributed. Diffusion occurs when two different particle concentrations are adjacent.

The difference in concentration which causes diffusion is called a *concentration gradient*. The greater the concentration gradient, the greater is the rate of diffusion. If no concentration gradient exists, diffusion does not occur, and the situation

high particle concentration — low particle concentration

direction of particle movement

diffusion

is described as *equilibrium*.

Diffusion is the method by which many substances enter and leave living organisms, and are transported within and between **cells**. Examples are (a) uptake of water by plants from **soil**, (b) **gas exchange** between plants and the atmosphere, and (c) gas exchange between **blood** and respiring cells.

Where diffusion is too slow for a particular function, substances can be transported more rapidly by **active transport**. For a special case of diffusion see **osmosis**.

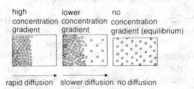

high concentration gradient	lower concentration gradient	no concentration gradient (equilibrium)
rapid diffusion	slower diffusion	no diffusion

diffusion Concentration gradients and equilibrium.

digestion The breakdown by **enzyme** action of large insoluble food particles into small soluble particles, prior to **absorption** and **assimilation**. In many animals, including mammals, digestion and absorption occur in the **alimentary canal**. See table on page 70.

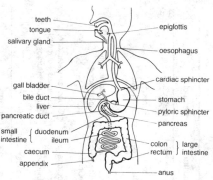

digestion The human alimentary canal.

Labels: teeth, tongue, salivary gland, gall bladder, bile duct, liver, pancreatic duct, small intestine {duodenum, ileum}, caecum, appendix, epiglottis, oesophagus, cardiac sphincter, stomach, pyloric sphincter, pancreas, colon, rectum} large intestine, anus

diploid Describing a **nucleus, cell** or organism in which the full complement of **chromosomes** is present, these occurring in pairs of **homologous chromosomes**. All animal cells, except **gametes**, are diploid, since gametes contain half the diploid number (**haploid**) as the result of **meiosis**. See **fertilization, haploid, mitosis**.

disaccharides Double **sugar carbohydrates** consisting of two **monosaccharides** linked together by bonds. For example, maltose is two **glucose** units joined together, while *sucrose* is

Location	Glands	Enzyme	Substrate	Product
Mouth	Salivary	Amylase	Starch	Maltose
Stomach	Gastric	Pepsin	Protein	Peptides
		Rennin	Milk protein	Coagulated milk
Duodenum	Pancreas	Amylase	Starch	Maltose
		Lipase	Fats	Fatty acids+glycerol
		Trypsin	Protein+peptides	Amino acids
Ileum		Lactase	Lactose	Glucose+galactose
		Lipase	Fats	Fatty acids+glycerol
		Maltase	Maltose	Glucose+fructose
		Peptidase	Peptides	Amino acids

digestion Digestive enzymes in humans.

one glucose unit linked with one *fructose* unit.

disaccharides Chemical structure.

disinfectant A chemical used to kill **microbes** outside the body, for example on surfaces such as floors.

division A unit used in the **classification** of plants. It is the equivalent of the term **phylum** used in the classification of animals. Divisions and phyla consist of one or more **classes**.

DNA (deoxyribonucleic acid) Nucleic acid which is the major constituent of **genes** and hence **chromosomes**. DNA consists of a double *polynucleotide* chain, twisted into a *helix*, the two chains being held together by bonds between nitrogen *base pairs*.

The nitrogen bases can only link as complementary pairs: *thymine* with *adenine* and *guanine* with *cytosine*. The numbers and sequence of base pairs in the DNA polynucleotide chain represent coded information (the **genetic code**) which acts as a blueprint for the transfer

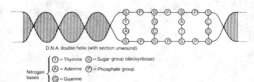

D.N.A. double helix (with section unwound)

Nitrogen bases
$\begin{cases} \text{(T)} = \text{Thymine} \\ \text{(A)} = \text{Adenine} \\ \text{(G)} = \text{Guanine} \\ \text{(C)} = \text{Cytosine} \end{cases}$
$\begin{array}{l} \text{(S)} = \text{Sugar group (deoxyribose)} \\ \text{(P)} = \text{Phosphate group.} \end{array}$

DNA Structure of the double helix.

of hereditary information from generation to generation.

DNA replication During **mitosis**, the formation of two new molecules of **DNA**, each of which has exactly the same sequence of bases as the parent molecule. The process requires the four *nucleotides*, the appropriate **enzymes** and **ATP** for **energy**.

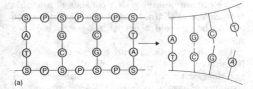

(a)

DNA replication (a) The DNA double chain unwinds and unzips.

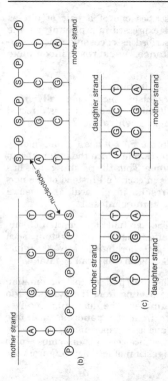

DNA replication (b) Each single chain then links with the appropriate nucleotide raw materials which are available in the **cell**. (c) After attachment of the bases, enzymes link the adjacent (S) and (P) molecules into two DNA double chains which are identical to each other and to the original 'mother' chain.

dominant Describes one of a pair of **alleles** which is always expressed in a **phenotype**, the other being described as **recessive**. See **monohybrid inheritance, backcross, incomplete dominance**.

dorsal Describes features of, on, or near, that surface of an organism which is normally directed upwards, although in humans it is directed backwards. Compare **ventral**.

Down's syndrome A human abnormality caused by a **mutation** in which the **ovum** has an extra **chromosome**. Thus the resulting child has 47 chromosomes in each **cell** instead of the normal 46. This results in physical and mental retardation. See **amniocentesis**.

drug abuse The habitual consumption of substances which affect the **nervous system**. Such drugs include LSD, heroin and solvents (glue-sniffing). Overdosing on drugs can be fatal.

duodenum The first part of the mammalian **small intestine** leading from the **stomach** via the pyloric **sphincter**. The duodenum receives *pancreatic juice* from the **pancreas** and **bile** from the **liver**, and is an important digestive site.

The pancreatic juice contains **enzymes** which continue the **digestion** of food arriving from the stomach.

$$\text{Starch} \xrightarrow{\text{Amylase}} \text{Maltose}$$

$$\text{Protein} \xrightarrow{\text{Trypsin}} \text{Peptides} \longrightarrow \begin{array}{l}\text{Amino}\\\text{acids}\end{array}$$

$$\text{Fat} \xrightarrow{\text{Lipase}} \text{Fatty acids} + \text{Glycerol}$$

Bile contains *bile salts* which emulsify fat, forming small fat droplets, thus increasing the surface area available for **lipase** action.

From the duodenum, the semidigested food is forced by **peristalsis** into the **ileum**.

ear The **organ** of hearing and balance in vertebrates. Hearing is a sensation produced by vibrations or sound waves which are converted into **nerve impulses** by the ear and transmitted to the **brain**.

Outer ear: the **pinna** is a funnel-shaped structure which directs sound waves into the ear and along the **auditory canal**, at the end of which is a very thin membrane, the *eardrum* (**tympanum**), which is made to vibrate by the sound waves.

Middle ear: this is an air-filled cavity connected to the back of the mouth (**pharynx**) by the **eustachian tube**, an arrangement which allows air into the middle ear ensuring equal air press-

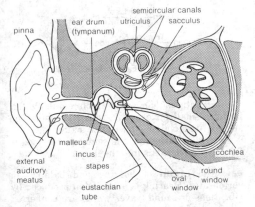

ear Structure of the human ear.

ure on both sides of the eardrum.

Within the middle ear, there are three tiny bones, the **ossicles**, named by their shapes: *malleus* (hammer), *incus* (anvil), and *stapes* (stirrup).

The vibrations of the eardrum are transmitted through and amplified by the ossicles, the stapes finally vibrating against a membrane called the **oval window**, which separates the middle and inner ears.

Inner ear: this is fluid-filled and consists of the **cochlea** and **semicircular canals**.

The vibration of the stapes against the **oval window** sets up waves in the fluid of the cochlea. These waves stimulate **receptor cells** (*hair cells*) causing nerve impulses to be sent via the **auditory nerve** to the brain, where they are interpreted as sounds.

Balance is maintained by the semicircular canals in association with information received from the **eyes** and **muscles**. The semicircular canals contain fluid and receptor cells, which are stimulated by movements of the fluid during changes in posture. The nerve impulses initiated by these cells travel to the brain along the auditory nerve and trigger **responses** which cause the body to maintain normal posture.

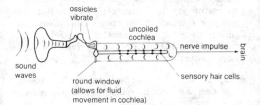

ear Sound waves are converted into nerve impulses.

ecdysis See **exoskeleton**.

ecology The study of the ways in which **communities** of plants and animals interact with one another and with their nonliving **environment**. See **ecosystem**.

ecosystem A **community** of organisms interacting with each other and with their nonliving **environment**, i.e. it is a natural unit consisting of living parts (plants and animals) and nonliving parts (light, water, air, etc.).

Habitat+Community→Ecosystem

Ecosystems can be lakes, ocean, forests, etc. The driving force behind all ecosystems is the flow of energy originating from the sun.

ecosystem management The use of good management practices in order to conserve the **environment**, for example, by taking the appropriate measures to reduce **pollution**, controlling the use of **fertilizers** and **pesticides** and adopting sensible methods of **agriculture** such as **crop rotation**.

ectoparasite A **parasite** living on the exterior of its *host*. *Lice* are an example of ectoparasites. See **endoparasite**.

effector A specialized animal **tissue** or **organ** that performs a **response** to a **stimulus** from the **environment**. Examples are **muscles** and

endocrine glands. See **sensitivity**.

electron See **atom**.

element A pure chemical that cannot be broken down into simpler substances. All the **atoms** of an element have the same number of **protons** or **electrons**. There are 92 naturally occurring elements.

embryo 1. A young animal developed from a **zygote** as a result of repeated **cell division**. In mammals, the embryo develops within the female **uterus**, and in the later stages of **pregnancy** is called a **foetus**.
2. A young flowering plant developed from a fertilized **ovule**, which in *seed plants* is enclosed within a **seed**, prior to **germination**.

embryo sac The structure within the **ovules** of flowering plants in which the female **gametes** are located. See **carpel**.

endocrine (ductless) glands Structures which release chemicals called **hormones** directly into the bloodstream in vertebrates and some invertebrates. The rate of secretion of hormones is often a response to changes in internal body conditions but may also be a response to changes in the **environment**. Compare **exocrine glands**. See diagram on page 80.

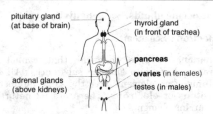

pituitary gland (at base of brain)

thyroid gland (in front of trachea)

pancreas

ovaries (in females)

adrenal glands (above kidneys)

testes (in males)

endocrine glands The main endocrine glands in the human body.

endoparasite A **parasite** living inside the body of its *host*. An example is the *tapeworm*. See **ectoparasite**.

endoskeleton or **internal skeleton** The **skeleton** lying within an animal's body, for example, the bony skeleton of vertebrates. Endoskeletons provide shape, support, and protection and in concert with **muscles** produce movement. Compare **exoskeleton**.

energy The ability to do work. In living organisms that work is done in performing the seven characteristics of life: movement, feeding, **reproduction**, **excretion**, **growth**, **sensitivity**, **respiration**.

Types of energy are: heat, light, sound, electrical, chemical, nuclear, potential (stored), and

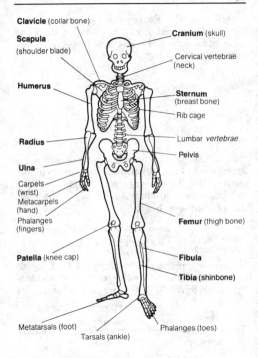

Clavicle (collar bone)

Scapula
(shoulder blade)

Humerus

Radius

Ulna

Carpels
(wrist)
Metacarpels
(hand)
Phalanges
(fingers)

Patella (knee cap)

Cranium (skull)

Cervical vertebrae
(neck)

Sternum
(breast bone)

Rib cage

Lumbar *vertebrae*

Pelvis

Femur (thigh bone)

Fibula

Tibia (shinbone)

Metatarsals (foot)

Tarsals (ankle)

Phalanges (toes)

endoskeleton The human endoskeleton.

kinetic (moving). Energy can neither be created nor destroyed, but it can be changed from one form into another. This scientific law is called the *conservation of energy*. Examples:

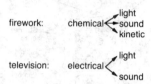

firework: chemical
- light
- sound
- kinetic

television: electrical
- light
- sound

This concept of energy interconversion is important to living organisms, since green plants convert the light energy of sunlight into the chemical/potential energy of food, via the reaction of **photosynthesis**.

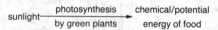

$$\text{sunlight} \xrightarrow[\text{by green plants}]{\text{photosynthesis}} \text{chemical/potential energy of food}$$

Other organisms can then release that chemical/potential energy via the reaction of **respiration** and convert it into other useful forms. For example:

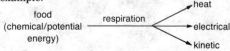

food
(chemical/potential   respiration
energy)
- heat
- electrical
- kinetic

environment The surroundings in which

organisms live and which influence the distribution and success of organisms. Many factors contribute to the environment, including (a) non-living **abiotic factors**, e.g. temperature, light, **pH** etc., and (b) living **biotic factors**, e.g. **predators**, **competition**.

The interaction of these factors determines the conditions within **habitats**, and 'selects' the **communities** of organisms which are best suited to these conditions.

enzymes Proteins which act as *catalysts* within cells. Catalysts are substances which cause chemical reactions to proceed, and in cells there may be hundreds of reactions occurring, each one requiring a particular enzyme.

$$A + B \xrightarrow{\quad\quad} X \longrightarrow \text{no reaction}$$

$$A + B \xrightarrow{\text{enzyme}} C + D$$

reactants   products

Enzymes catalyse either *synthesis* by which complex compounds are formed from simple mol-

enzymes The synthesis and degradation of starch.

ecules, or *degradation* by which complex molecules are broken down to simple subunits by **hydrolysis**. See **digestion**.

Enzyme characteristics
(a) Enzymes are **proteins**.
(b) Enzymes work most efficiently within a narrow temperature range. Thus human enzymes work best at 37°C (body temperature) and this is called the optimum temperature. Above and below this temperature their efficiency decreases, and at temperatures above 45°C most enzymes are destroyed (**denaturation**).

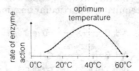

enzymes Graph showing the effect of substrate upon the rate of enzyme activity.

(c) Enzymes have an optimum **pH** at which they work most efficiently. For example, the **saliva** enzyme **salivary amylase** works best at neutral or slightly acid pH. The **stomach** enzyme **pepsin** will only function in an acid pH, while the enzyme **trypsin** in the

intestine favours an alkaline pH.

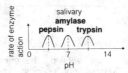

enzymes Graph showing the effect of pH upon enzyme activity.

(d) The rate of an enzyme-catalysed reaction increases as the enzyme concentration increases.

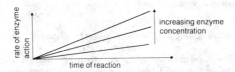

enzymes Graph showing the effect of substrate concentration upon the rate of reaction.

(e) The rate of an enzyme-catalysed reaction increases as the **substrate** concentration increases, up to a maximum point.

(f) Normally an enzyme will catalyse only one particular reaction, a property called specificity. For example, the enzyme *catalase* can

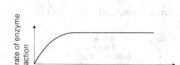

enzymes Graph showing the effect of substrate concentration upon the rate of reaction.

only degrade the compound *hydrogen peroxide*.

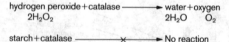

hydrogen peroxide + catalase $\longrightarrow$ water + oxygen
$2H_2O_2$ $2H_2O$ O_2

starch + catalase $\longrightarrow\!\!\!\times\!\!\!\longrightarrow$ No reaction

Naming enzymes. Most enzymes are named by adding the suffix *-ase* to the name of the enzyme's substrate. For example, **maltase** acts on maltose; urease acts on **urea**, etc.

enzyme mechanism Enzyme action is explained by the 'lock and key hypothesis' in which the enzyme is thought of as a lock into which only certain keys (the substrate molecules) can fit. In this way, the enzyme and the substrate are brought together and the reaction can occur.

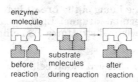

enzyme
molecule

before
reaction

substrate
molecules
during reaction

after
reaction

enzyme mechanism Sequence illustrating an enzyme-catalysed synthesis. Reversing the order of the diagrams shows how an enzyme-catalysed degradation occurs.

epidermis The protective outermost layer of **cells** in an animal or plant. The epidermis of many **multicellular** invertebrates is one cell thick and is often covered with a **cuticle**. In most vertebrates, the epidermis is the outer layer of **skin**, and in land vertebrates may have several layers of dead cells. In plants, the epidermis is one cell thick, and on aerial structures may have a cuticle. See **leaf**, **root**, **stem**.

epiglottis The flap of **cartilage** and membrane at the base of the tongue on the ventral wall of the **pharynx**. It closes the **trachea** during swallowing. See **digestion**.

epithelium Lining **tissue** in vertebrates consisting of closely packed layers of **cells**, covering internal and external surfaces. For example, the

skin and the lining of the **breathing**, digestive and urinogenital **organs**. Epithelia may also contain specialized structures, e.g. **cilia**, **goblet cells**.

erythrocyte See **red blood cell**.

eustachian tube The tube connecting the **middle ear** to the **pharynx** in tetrapods. It is important in equalizing air pressure on either side of the **eardrum**. See **ear**.

evolution The development of complex organisms from simpler ancestors occurring over successive generations. See **natural selection.**

excretion Elimination of the waste products of **metabolism** by living organisms. The main excretory products are water, carbon dioxide and nitrogenous compounds, e.g. **urea**. In simple organisms excretion occurs through the **cell membrane** or **epidermis**, in higher plants via the **leaves**, while most animals have specialized excretory **organs**. For example, in man the **lungs** excrete water and carbon dioxide, and the **kidneys** excrete urea.

exercise Any physical activity or bodily exertion which contributes to good health. Evidence suggests that regular exercise reduces the risk of **heart** disease, probably as a result of improved

blood circulation. See **circulatory system**.

exocrine glands Structures in vertebrates which release secretions to **epithelial** surfaces via **ducts** e.g. *sweat glands*; *salivary glands*. Compare **endocrine glands**.

exoskeleton or **external skeleton** A **skeleton** lying outside the body of some invertebrates, for example, the **cuticle** of insects and the shells of crabs. Some organisms shed and renew their exoskeletons periodically to allow **growth**, a process known as *moulting* or **ecdysis**. Compare **endoskeleton**.

(a)

(b)

exoskeleton The exoskeletons of (a) an insect and (b) a crustacean.

eye A **sense organ** responding to light, ranging from very simple structures in invertebrates to the complex organs of insects and vertebrates. Eye muscles enable the eye to move up and down and from side to side.

The **sclerotic** is a tough protective layer which

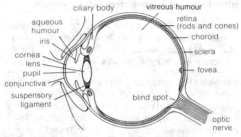

eye Vertical section through the human eye.

at the front of the eye forms the transparent **cornea**.

The **choroid** is a black-pigmented layer under the sclerotic, rich in **blood vessels** supplying food and oxygen to the eye.

The **retina** is a layer of **nerve cells** which are sensitive to light. There are two types of cells in the retina, named by their shape:

(a) **Rods** are very sensitive to low intensity light and are particularly concentrated in the eyes of nocturnal animals;

(b) **Cones** are sensitive to bright light. There are different types which are stimulated by different wavelengths of light and are thus responsible for *colour vision*. Animals whose retinas lack cones are colour blind, while human colour blindness is caused by a defect in the cones.

The **fovea** (*yellow spot*) is a small area of the retina containing only cones in great concentration and giving the greatest degree of detail and colour.

The **blind spot** is that part of the retina at which **nerve fibres** connected to the rods and cones leave the eye to enter the **optic nerve** which leads to the **brain**. Since there are no light-sensitive cells at this point, an image formed at the blind spot is not registered by the brain.

The **lens** is a transparent biconvex structure which can change curvature.

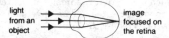

light
from an
object

image
focused on
the retina

eye   The lens focuses light on the retina.

The lens is held in place by **suspensory ligaments** which are attached to the **ciliary muscles**, the contraction or relaxation of which alters the shape of the lens, allowing both near and distant objects to be focused sharply. This is called **accommodation**.

The **iris** is the coloured part of the eye, containing **muscles** which vary the size of the *pupil*, the hole through which light enters the eye. In poor light, the pupils are wide open (dilated), to increase the brightness of the image. In bright light the pupils are contracted to protect the retina from possible damage. This mechanism is an example of a **reflex action**.

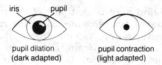

iris   pupil

pupil dilation   pupil contraction
(dark adapted)   (light adapted)

eye The pupil dilates and contracts according to the intensity of the light.

Because the pupil is small, light rays enter the eye in such a way that the image at the retina is upside down (inverted). This inversion of the image is corrected by the brain.

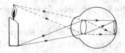

eye The image is smaller than the object, and is inverted.

The **aqueous** and **vitreous humours** are fluids which fill the chambers of the eye. They help to maintain shape, focus light, and allow nutrients, oxygen, and wastes to diffuse to and from the eye **cells**.

F₁ generation (first filial generation) The first generation of **progeny** obtained in breeding experiments. Successive generations are called F_2 etc. See **monohybrid inheritance**.

faeces In vertebrates, the solid or semisolid remains of undigested food, **bacteria**, etc, which are formed in the **colon** and expelled via the **anus**.

family The unit used in the **classification** of living organisms consisting of one or more genera (singular **genus**).

fats or lipids **Organic compounds** containing the elements carbon, hydrogen, oxygen. Fats consist of three *fatty acid* molecules (which may be the same or different) bonded to one glycerol molecule.

Fat deposits under the **skin** act as long term **energy** stores, yielding 39 kJ/g when respired;

fats Structure of a fat molecule.

these deposits also provide heat insulation.

Fat is an important constituent of the **cell membrane** and its insolubility in water is utilized in the waterproofing systems of many organisms. See **respiration**.

femur 1. Part of insect limb nearest to the body. 2. The thighbone of **tetrapod** vertebrates. See **endoskeleton**.

fermentation The degradation of **organic compounds** in the absence of oxygen for the purpose of **energy** production, by certain organisms, particularly **bacteria** and **yeasts**. Fermentation is a form of anaerobic **respiration**. See **brewing**.

$$\text{glucose} \xrightarrow[\text{ADP}]{\text{yeast}} \text{ethanol} + \text{carbon dioxide}$$

$$\begin{array}{cccc} \text{glucose} & & \text{ethanol} & + \text{ carbon dioxide} \\ C_6H_{12}O_6 & & 2C_2H_5OH & 2CO_2 \\ \text{ADP} & \textbf{ATP} & & \end{array}$$

fermentation The fermentation of sugars by yeast produces the by-products ethanol and carbon dioxide.

fertilization The fusing of **haploid gametes** during **sexual reproduction** resulting in a single cell, the **zygote**, containing the **diploid** number of chromosomes.

External fertilization occurs when the gametes

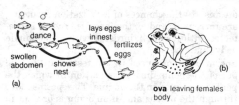

ova leaving females body

(a) (b)

fertilization External fertilization in (a) fish: the stickleback and (b) amphibians: the toad.

are passed out of the parents and fertilization and development take place independently of the parents. External fertilization is common in aquatic organisms where the movement of water helps the gametes to meet.

Internal fertilization is particularly associated with terrestrial animals, for example, insects, birds and mammals, and involves the union of the gametes within the female's body. The advantages of internal fertilization are (a) the **sperms** are not exposed to unfavourable dry con-

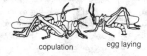

copulation   egg laying

fertilization Internal fertilization in an insect: the locust.

ditions, (b) the chances of fertilization occurring are increased, and (c) the fertilized **ovum** is protected within a shell (birds) or within the female body (mammals).

Sperm cells, produced in the testes, are passed out of the penis during copulation in which the penis is inserted in the vagina. The sperms move through the uterus and, if an ovum is present in an oviduct, fertilization can occur there.

Fertilization of ovum. The fertilized ovum (**zygote**) continues moving towards the uterus, dividing repeatedly as it does so. On arrival at

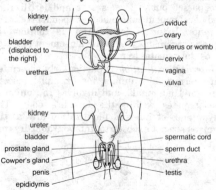

fertilization The human reproductive organs.

the uterus, the zygote, by now a ball of cells, becomes embedded in the prepared wall of the uterus. This is called **implantation** and further development of the **embryo** occurs in the uterus. See **pregnancy, birth**.

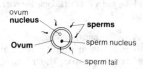

fertilization   Fertilization of the ovum.

Fertilization in plants. In flowering plants, after **pollination**, **pollen** grains deposited on *stigmas* absorb nutrients and *pollen tubes* grow down through the *style* and enter the ovules

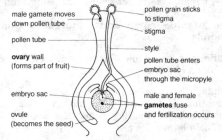

fertilization   Fertilization in plants.

through the **micropyles**. The tip of each pollen tube breaks down and the male **gamete** enters the ovule and fuses with the female gamete.

After fertilization, the ovule, containing the plant embryo, develops into a **seed**, and the **ovary** develops into a **fruit**. See **flower**, **pollen**, **pollination**.

fertilizer Any substance added to **soil** to increase the quantity or quality of plant growth. When crops are harvested, the natural circulation of soil **mineral salts** is disturbed, i.e., mineral salts absorbed by plants are not returned to soil. This is called **soil depletion** and may render the soil infertile. Fertilizers replenish the soil and are of two types:

(a) Organic fertilizers such as sewage;
(b) Inorganic fertilizers such as ammonium sulphate.

See **organic compounds**, **inorganic compounds**.

fibrinogen A soluble **plasma protein** involved in **blood clotting**.

fibula The posterior of two **bones** in the lower hind-limb of **tetrapods**. In humans it is the outer bone of the leg below the knee. See **endoskeleton**.

fitness The state of being in healthy physical

condition. Fitness is achieved and maintained by adopting a healthy lifestyle, for example by having a **balanced diet** and taking regular **exercise**, and avoiding alcohol, smoking and drug abuse.

flagellum A microscopic motile thread projecting from certain **cell** surfaces and causing movement by lashing back and forth. Flagella are usually larger than **cilia**, and less numerous, and are responsible for locomotion in many **unicellular** organisms and reproductive cells.

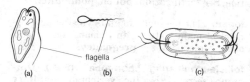

flagella

(a)   (b)   (c)

flagellum Flagella in (a) *Euglena* (b) motile sperm (c) motile bacterium.

flower The organ of **sexual reproduction** in flowering plants (angiosperms).

Insect-pollinated flowers have brightly coloured and scented petals, and usually have a nectary. The stamens and carpels (with sticky **stigmas**) are within the flower. These adaptations favour insect pollination.

Wind-pollinated flowers are small, often green

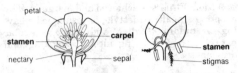

flower The structure of (a) an insect-pollinated flower, (b) a wind-pollinated flower.

and unscented, and do not have nectaries. The anthers and feathery stigmas dangle out of the flowers when ripe thus facilitating wind pollination. See **fertilization, pollen, pollination**.

foetus The mammalian **embryo** after development of main features. In humans this is after about three months of **pregnancy**.

follicle-stimulating hormone (FSH) Hormone secreted by the vertebrate **pituitary gland**. See **ovulation**.

food calorimeter A device for measuring the **energy** content of food.
A weighed food sample is ignited using the heating filament. In the presence of oxygen, the food sample is completely combusted, the released energy being transferred to the surrounding water, which shows a rise in temperature.
From this rise in temperature, it is possible to calculate the energy content of the food in

food	energy content
protein	17 kJ/g
carbohydrate	17 kJ/g
fat	39 kJ/g

kilojoules per gram (kJ/g).

Note: the kilojoule has replaced the calorie as the unit of energy.

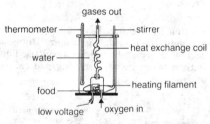

food calorimeter

food capture Many **heterotrophic** organisms have developed very specialized methods and structures for obtaining food; a variety of examples is given below.

(a) Mammals without teeth. Anteaters have a long and sticky tongue for catching ants. Blue whales have modified mouth parts to filter

plankton out of water.

(b) Filter feeding. Like the blue whale, many aquatic organisms filter plankton.

food capture   Filter feeding: *Mytilus* (the edible mussel) shown with one shell removed.

(c) Feeding by sucking. Houseflies pass **saliva** out onto their food, e.g. sugar. **Digestion** begins immediately and the resulting liquid is then taken in by a sucking pad called a *proboscis*.

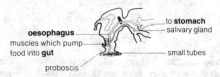

food capture   The housefly sucks up dissolved food.

Female mosquitoes pierce the human skin, inject a fluid which prevents **blood clotting**,

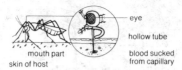

food capture The female mosquito sucks blood.

and then suck up some blood. This feeding mechanism can cause the disease malaria, since the **parasite** involved may be transmitted during feeding.

Butterflies feed on the nectar produced by flowering plants. They suck the nectar from the

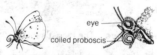

food capture The butterfly's long coil proboscis.

flower by means of a long tube-like proboscis, which remains coiled when not in use.

Greenflies use a long piercing proboscis to suck plant juices from **leaves** and **stems**.

(d) Biting without teeth. Locusts eat their own weight of plant material every day. They have powerful biting jaws called *mandibles*

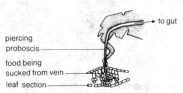

food capture   The greenfly's proboscis.

which have very hard biting edges, which are brought together during feeding in a precise and efficient shearing action. See **carnivore**, **dentition**, **herbivore**, **omnivore**.

mandibles

food capture   The locust's biting jaws.

food chain A food relationship in which **energy** and carbon compounds obtained by green plants via **photosynthesis** are passed to other living organisms, i.e., plants are eaten by animals which in turn are eaten by other animals and so on.

The arrows indicate 'is eaten by'. An example of such a food chain is:

plants→insects→lizards→snakes

Not all food chains are as long as the above, for example:

grass→sheep→man
grass→antelope→lion

Such simple food chains seldom exist independently; more often several food chains are linked in a more complicated relationship called a *food web*.

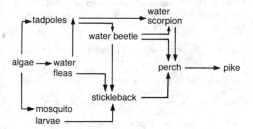

food chain Part of the food web in a freshwater pond.

All food webs are delicately balanced. Should one link in the web be destroyed, all the other organisms will be affected. For example, in the pond food web, if the perch disappeared as the result of disease, the pike population would decrease while the water scorpions would increase.

food consumers Heterotrophic organisms which, after green plants, occupy the subsequent links in a **food chain**.

food producers Autotrophic organisms, mainly green plants, which occupy the first level in a **food chain**.

food tests Chemical tests used to identify the components of a food sample. Some common food tests are shown below.

protein	+	Biuret reagent (blue)	→	violet/purple colour
reducing sugar	+	Benedict's reagent (blue)	→ heat	green/yellow/brick red colour
starch	+	iodine solution (brown)	→	blue/black colour
fat	+ water	+ ethanol (clear)	→	white emulsion
vitamin C	+	dichlorophenolindo-phenol (DCPIP) (blue)	→	DCPIP (clear)

food web See **food chain**.

fossil The hardened remains of animal and plant **tissue** from previous geological ages, which have been preserved in the earth's crust. The study of fossils is called **palaeontology**, and has supplied important evidence for **evolution**.

fossil fuels The fossilised remains of plants and animals which, over millions of years, have been transformed into oil, coal and natural gas. See **carbon cycle**, **greenhouse effect**.

fovea or **yellow spot** Area of the **retina** in some vertebrate **eyes**, specialized for acute vision. It contains numerous **cones** but no **rods**.

fruit The ripened **ovary** of a **flower**, enclosing **seeds**, formed as the result of **pollination** and **fertilization**. The fruit protects the seed and aids its dispersal.

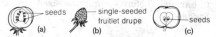

    fruit (a) tomato (b) blackberry (c) apple.

fruit and seed dispersal The methods by which most flowering plants spread seeds far away from the parent plant, thus (a) avoiding **competition** for resources and (b) ensuring wide colonization, so that suitable **habitats** are likely to be encountered by a proportion of seeds. The methods are:

(a) Wind dispersal. Air currents carry the fruits or seeds which usually show an adaptation to increase surface area.

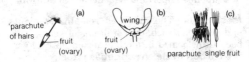

fruit Methods of wind dispersal: (a) dandelion (b) sycamore (c) groundsel.

(b) Animal dispersal. Hooked fruits, e.g. burdock, stick to animals' coats and may be brushed off some distance from the parent plant. Succulent berries, for example, the strawberry, are eaten by animals, and the small hard fruits containing seeds pass through the **gut** unharmed before being released in the **faeces**.

fruit Examples of fruit dispersed by animals: (a) burdock (b) strawberry.

(c) Explosive dispersal. Unequal drying of part of a fruit causes the fruit to burst.

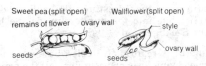

Sweet pea (split open)   Wallflower (split open)

remains of flower   ovary wall   style

seeds   ovary wall   seeds

fruit Sweet pea and wallflower disperse their seeds by explosion of the fruit.

FSH See **follicle-stimulating hormone**.

fungi A **heterotrophic** plant group which includes the microscopic *moulds* and **yeasts** such as *Mucor* and *Penicillium* and also the **multicellular** *mushrooms* and *toadstools*. Some fungi are **parasites** causing plant disease such as potato blight and Dutch elm disease. In humans, fungi cause athletes foot, ringworm and **lung** infections. Other fungi are useful to man, for example as a source of **antibiotics** and in **brewing**.

spores

sporangium   developing sporangium

hypha

(a)   (b)

fungi (a) *Mucor* (b) *Penecillium*.

gall bladder A small bladder in or near the vertebrate **liver**, in which **bile** is stored. When food enters the **intestine**, the gall bladder empties bile into the **duodenum** via the **bile duct**. See **digestion**.

gamete A reproductive **cell** whose nucleus is formed by **meiosis** and contains half the normal **chromosome** number (**haploid**). Human male gametes are **spermatozoa** and the female gametes are **ova** (egg cells). Male and female gametes fuse during **fertilization** forming a **zygote** in which the normal chromosome number (**diploid**) is restored.

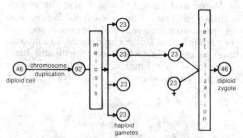

gamete In humans, the haploid gametes have 23 chromosomes and the diploid zygote has 46.

gametophyte Phase in the **life cycle** of a plant that bears **gamete**-producing organs. In plants that demonstrate **alternation of generations** it may or may not be the dominant phase, but arises from the development of a **haploid spore** from the **sporophyte** generation.

gas exchange The process by which organisms exchange gases with the **environment** for the purpose of **metabolism**. Most organisms require a continuous supply of the gas oxygen for the reaction of **respiration**:

$$\textbf{glucose} + \text{oxygen} \rightarrow \textbf{energy} + \text{carbon} + \text{water}$$
$$\text{dioxide}$$

In addition, green plants require carbon dioxide for the reaction of **photosynthesis**:

$$\text{carbon} + \text{water} \xrightarrow[\text{chlorophyll}]{\substack{\text{light} \\ \text{energy}}} \textbf{carbohydrate} + \text{oxygen}$$
$$\text{dioxide}$$

Both reactions use and produce gases which are interchanged between the atmosphere (land organisms) or water (aquatic organisms).

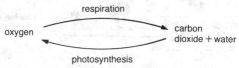

gas exchange Both respiration and photosynthesis involve gas exchange with the environment.

Gas-exchange surfaces. Gas exchange takes place across surfaces which have the following characteristics:

(a) A large surface area for maximum gas exchange;

(b) The surface is thin to allow easy **diffusion**;

(c) The surface is moist since gas exchange occurs in solution;

(d) In animals, the surface has a good blood supply, since the gases involved are transported via the **blood**.

Gas exchange in fish occurs across **gills** which consist of *gill arches* to which are attached numerous gill filaments. Water is taken in via the mouth and passed over the gills where oxygen dissolved in the water is absorbed into **blood capillaries** while carbon dioxide diffuses into the water.

Gas exchange in insects: air enters insects

(gill cover removed)

deoxygenated blood→ from **heart**

gill filaments

gill arch

oxygenated blood← for body

gas exchange The position and structure of the gills of fish.

through pores called **spiracles** and is carried through a branching system of **tracheae** and thus into smaller branches called *tracheoles* which are in contact with the **tissues**.

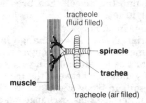

gas exchange Gas exchange in insects occurs via the fluid in the tracheoles.

Gas exchange in mammals occurs as the result of **concentration gradients** existing between the

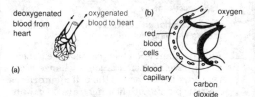

gas exchange (a) Alveoli and associated blood vessels. (b) Gas exchange in the alveolus.

air in the alveoli and the *deoxygenated* **blood** arriving from the **heart**. These gradients cause **diffusion** of oxygen from the alveoli into **red blood cells** and diffusion of carbon dioxide from the **blood** into the alveoli. See **breathing (in mammals), lungs**.

Gas exchange in plants:

(a) Terrestrial plants. **Gas exchange** in **leaves** and young **stems** occurs through pores in the **epidermis** called **stomata**. In young **roots** it occurs by diffusion between the roots and air in the **soil**. In older stems and roots where bark has formed, gas exchange takes place through gaps in the bark called lenticels.

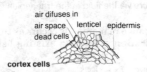

air difuses in
air space   lenticel   epidermis
dead cells
cortex cells

gas exchange Section through plant stem showing lenticel.

(b) Aquatic plants. Submerged plants, e.g. pondweed, have no stomata, gas exchange occurring by diffusion across the **cell membranes**. Aquatic plants with floating leaves, e.g. water lily, have stomata only on the upper leaf surface.

(c) *Nongreen plants*. Mushrooms, for example,

carry out **respiration** but not **photosynthesis**. Gas exchange occurs by diffusion between the plant cells and the surrounding air.

gastric Describes parts and functions of the body related to the **stomach**.

genes The subunits of **chromosomes** consisting of lengths of **DNA** which control the hereditary characteristics of organisms. Genes consist of up to one thousand **base pairs** in a DNA molecule, the particular sequence of which represents coded information. This is known as the **genetic code** and determines the types of **proteins** synthesized by **cells**, particularly **enzymes**, which then dictate the structure and function of cells and **tissues**, and ultimately organisms, i.e., a cell or an organism is an expression of the genes it has inherited (and the **environment** in which it lives).

The genetic code is the arrangement of nitrogen base pairs in DNA. Each group of three adjacent base pairs (triplets) is responsible for linking together, within the cell, **amino acids** to form protein. The sequence, types and numbers of amino acids determine the nature of the proteins, which in turn determine the characteristics of cells. For example, the base triplet GTA codes for the amino acid histidine while GTT codes for glutamine.

Consider two fruit flies (*Drosophila*), one with a gene X controlling body colour, while the other's body colour is controlled by gene Y.

gene X $\xrightarrow[\text{synthesizes}]{}$ enzyme X $\xrightarrow[\text{catalyses}]{}$ pigment X

gene Y $\xrightarrow[\text{synthesizes}]{}$ enzyme Y $\xrightarrow[\text{catalyses}]{}$ pigment Y

pigment X $\xrightarrow[\text{produces}]{}$ light body

pigment Y $\xrightarrow[\text{produces}]{}$ dark body

genetic code See **genes**.

genetic engineering The transfer of pieces of **chromosome** from one organism to another. For example, the **gene** for human **insulin** can be inserted into a **bacterium** which will then produce insulin that can be isolated and purified for treatment of diabetes. See diagram on opposite page.

genetics The study of *heredity*, which is the transmission of characteristics from parents to offspring via the **genes** in the **chromosomes**. Heredity is investigated by performing breeding experiments and then comparing the characteristics of the parents and offspring. Such experiments were first done by Gregor Mendel in the 1860s using pea plants. See **monohybrid inheritance**, **backcross**, **incomplete dominance**.

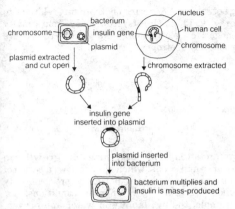

genetic engineering

genotype The genetic composition of an organism, i.e., the particular set of **alleles** in each cell. In breeding experiments, genotypes are represented by symbols, capital letters denoting the **dominant alleles** and small letters denoting the **recessive alleles**. See **monohybrid inheritance**.

genus A unit used in the **classification** of living organisms, consisting of a number of similar **species**.

geotropism A form of **tropism** relative to gravity. Plant **shoots** grow away from gravity (negative geotropism), but most **roots** are positively geotropic.

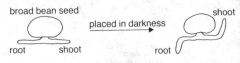

broad bean seed

placed in darkness

root   shoot

shoot

root

geotropism

germination The beginning of **growth** in **spores** and **seeds**, which often follows a period of *dormancy*, and which normally proceeds only under certain environmental conditions, for example, the availability of water and oxygen, and a favourable temperature. If these conditions are not present, spores and seeds may remain alive for some time before germinating. In this state, they are *dormant*.

Seed germination in flowering plants. There are two types of germination: hypogeal and epigeal. They are distinguished by what happens to the **cotyledons** during development of the seedling. In both cases water is absorbed via the **micropyle**, the **testa** splits open and the **radicle** emerges. See diagram on opposite page.

gestation period See **pregnancy**.

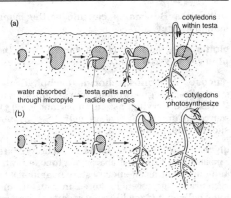

germination (a) Hypogeal germination (broad bean). (b) Epigeal germination (French bean).

gills The **gas-exchange surface** of aquatic animals. In fish, gills are usually internal, projecting from the **pharynx**, while in amphibian **larvae**, they are external. See **gas exchange**.

gland A cell or **organ** that synthesizes chemical substances and secretes them into the body either through a duct or direct to the bloodstream. See **endocrine gland**.

glomerulus The knot of **blood capillaries**

within the **Bowman's capsule** of the mammalian **kidney**.

glottis The opening of the **larynx** into the **pharynx** of vertebrates.

glucose A **monosaccharide carbohydrate**, synthesized in green plants, during **photosynthesis** and serving as an important **energy** source in animal and plant **cells**. See **monosaccharide**, **respiration**.

glycogen A **polysaccharide carbohydrate** consisting of branched chains of **glucose** units, and important as an **energy** store in animals. In vertebrates, glycogen is stored in **muscle** and **liver cells** and is readily converted to glucose by **amylase enzymes**. See **insulin**.

goblet cells Specialized **cells** in certain **epithelia**, which synthesize and secrete **mucus**. Goblet cells are common in vertebrates, and are found in, for example, the intestinal and respiratory tracts of mammals. See **intestine**.

epthelial cells

mucus-secreting goblet cells

goblet cells   Goblet cells in epithelium.

gonads   Organs in animals which produce **gametes** and in some cases **hormones**. Examples are the **ovaries** and **testes**.

Graafian follicle   A fluid-filled cavity in the mammalian **ovary** within which the **ovum** develops until **ovulation**.

greenhouse effect   The increase in global temperature caused by increasing atmospheric carbon dioxide levels. This has resulted from burning fossil fuels and the destruction of large areas of tropical forest (reduced **photosynthesis**). The increased carbon dioxide concentration traps the radiant **energy** of the sun in a similar way to a greenhouse and may result in the polar ice-caps melting and a rise in sea level.

growth   The increase in size and complexity of an organism during development from **embryo** to maturity, resulting from **cell division**, cell enlargement and **cell differentiation**. In plants, growth originates at certain localized areas called **meristems**, while animal growth goes on all over the body. See **primary growth, secondary growth**.

guard cells   Paired **cells** bordering **stomata** and controlling the opening and closing of the stomata. The **diffusion** of water into guard cells from adjacent **epidermis** cells causes the guard cells to expand and increase their **turgor**. However, they do not expand uniformly, the thicker, inelastic cell walls causing them to bend so that a pair of guard cells draws apart forming a stoma. Diffusion of water from guard cells reverses the process and closes the stoma. Stomata are normally open during the day and closed at night.

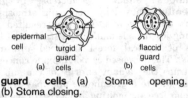

epidermal
cell
turgid   flaccid
guard   guard
(a) cells   (b) cells

guard cells (a) Stoma opening. (b) Stoma closing.

gut All or part of the **alimentary canal**.

gynaecium The collective name for the **carpels**, the female reproductive structures of a **flower**.

habitat The place where an animal or plant lives, the organism being adapted to the particular conditions within the habitat, which may be a sea-shore, pond, rockpool, etc. See **environment**.

haemoglobin Red pigment containing iron, within vertebrate **red blood cells**, responsible for the transport of oxygen throughout the body.

haemolysis The loss of **haemoglobin** from **red blood cells** as a result of damage to the **cell membrane**. This can be caused by several factors including **osmosis**, which can be investigated with human red blood cells which have a **solute** concentration equivalent to a 0.9 per cent sodium chloride solution.

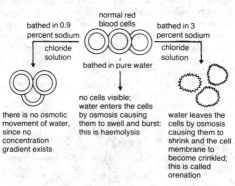

bathed in 0.9 percent sodium chloride solution

normal red blood cells

bathed in 3 percent sodium chloride solution

bathed in pure water

there is no osmotic movement of water, since no concentration gradient exists

no cells visible; water enters the cells by osmosis causing them to swell and burst: this is haemolysis

water leaves the cells by osmosis causing them to shrink and the cell membrane to become crinkled; this is called orenation

haemolysis Red blood cells in sodium chloride solution burst or shrink according to the concentration of the solution.

haemophilia See **sex linkage**.

haploid Describing a **nucleus**, **cell** or organism having a single set of unpaired **chromo-**

somes. The haploid number is found in plant and animal **gametes** as the result of **meiosis**. In plants with **alternation of generations**, the **spores** and **gametophyte** generation (gamete-producing stage) are haploid.

See **diploid**.

heart   A muscular pumping **organ** which maintains **blood** circulation, and is usually equipped with **valves** to prevent backward flow. In mammals, the heart has four chambers, consisting of two relatively thin-walled **atria** (or **auricles**) which receive blood, and two thicker-walled **ventricles** which pump blood out.

The right side of the heart deals only with

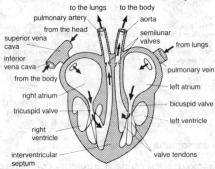

heart   Structure of the mammalian heart.

deoxygenated blood, and the left side only with oxygenated blood. The wall of the left ventricle is thicker and more powerful than that of the right, since it pumps all round the body, while the right ventricle pumps only to the lungs. See **circulatory system, heartbeat**.

heartbeat The alternative contraction and relaxation of the **heart**. In mammals it consists of two phases:

(a) *Diastole* The atria and **ventricles** relax, allowing **blood** to flow into the ventricles from the atria;

(b) *Systole* The ventricles contract, forcing blood into the **pulmonary artery** and **aorta**. The relaxed atria fill with blood in preparation for the next beat.

Heartbeat is initiated by a structure in the

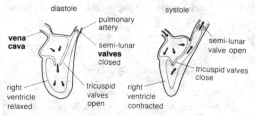

heartbeat Relaxation and contraction of heart (right side).

right atrium called the **pacemaker**, although the rate is controlled by the **medulla oblongata** of the **brain** which detects any increase in carbon dioxide in the blood as the result of increased **respiration** and is also affected by certain **hormones**, for example, **adrenalin** from the **adrenal gland**. The rate of human heartbeat is measured by counting **pulse rate**.

hepatic   Describes parts of the body related to the **liver** and its functions.

herbivore   An animal which feeds on plants. Herbivores include sheep, rabbits and cattle, and have a **dentition** adapted for chewing vegetation and a **gut** capable of **cellulose digestion**.

Most herbivore **teeth** are grinders; **canines** are usually absent. In herbivores without upper **incisors**, a horny pad of gum combines with the lower incisors in biting vegetation. In most

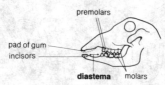

dental formula   incisors 0/4 ; canines 0/0 premolars ; 3/3
molars 3/3 (total : 32)

herbivore   The skull and teeth of a sheep.

herbivores the lower jaw can move sideways, or backwards and forwards, thus producing the grinding action of the teeth.

heterotrophic or **holozoic** Describing organisms which obtain **organic compounds** (food) by feeding on other organisms. Heterotrophs include all animals and **fungi**, most **bacteria** and a few flowering plants. Heterotrophs are also called **food consumers** and can be classified into **carnivores, herbivores, omnivores, saprophytes** and **parasites**. Compare **autotrophic**.

heterozygous Having two different **alleles** of the same **gene**. See **monohybrid inheritance**.

holophytic See **autotrophic**.

holozoic See **heterotrophic**.

homeostasis The maintenance of constant conditions within an organism. Examples are the control of **blood glucose** level by **insulin**, the control of blood water content by **ADH**, and the control of body temperature by the **skin**, etc.

homoiothermic Describes animals which maintain a constant narrow range of body temperature despite fluctuations in the **environ-**

ment. Mammals and birds are homoiothermic, although often described as *warm-blooded*. Compare **poikilothermic**; see **temperature regulation**.

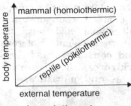

homoiothermic

homologous chromosomes Pairs of **chromosomes** that come together during **meiosis**. They carry **genes** that govern the same characteristics. Homologous pairs of chromosomes are found in all **diploid** organisms, one of the pair coming from the male **gamete** and the other from the female gamete, the pair being united at **fertilization**.

homozygous or **pure** Having two identical **alleles** for any one **gene**. See **monohybrid inheritance**.

hormones (animal) Chemicals secreted by the **endocrine glands** and transported via the

Endocrine gland	Hormone	Effects
Pituitary gland	ADH (anti-diuretic hormone)	Controls water reabsorption by the **kidneys**.
	TSH (thyroid stimulating hormone)	Stimulates thyroxine production in the thyroid gland.
	FSH (follicle-stimulating hormone)	Causes ova to mature and the ovaries to produce oestrogen.
	LH (luteinizing hormone)	Initiates ovulation and causes the ovaries to release progesterone.
	Growth hormone	Stimulates growth in young animals. In humans, deficiency causes dwarfism and excess causes gigantism.
Thyroid gland	Thyroxin	Controls rate of growth and development in young animals. In human infants, deficiency causes cretinism. Controls the rate of chemical activity in adults. Excess causes thinness and over-activity, and deficiency causes obesity and sluggishness.

Endocrine gland	Hormone	Effects
Pancreas (Islets of Langerhans	Insulin	Stimulates conversion of **glucose** to **glycogen** in the liver. Deficiency causes diabetes.
Adrenal glands	Adrenalin	Under conditions of 'fight, flight, or fright' causes changes which increase the efficiency of the animal. For example, increased heartbeat and breathing, diversion of blood from gut to muscles, conversion of glycogen in the liver to glucose.
Ovaries	Oestrogen	Stimulates secondary sexual characteristics in the female, for example, breast development. Causes the uterus wall to thicken during menstrual cycle.
	Progesterone	Prepares uterus for implantation.
Testes	Testosterone	Stimulates secondary sexual characteristics in the male, for example, facial hair.

bloodstream to certain **organs** (target organs) where they cause specific effects which are vital in regulating and coordinating body activities. Hormone action is usually slower than nervous stimulation. The following table summarizes the properties of some important human hormones; there are many others.

hormones (plant) Growth substances, for example, **auxins**, involved in many plant processes, including **tropisms, germination**, etc.

horticulture The science of plant growing which is of particular importance in food production.

human population curve A diagram showing changes in the human **population**. A population explosion has taken place in the last century due to improvements in food production and public health resulting in increasing **birth rate** and decreasing **death rate**. See diagram on page 132.

humerus Bone of the upper forelimb of **tetrapods**. In humans, the bone of the upper arm. See **endoskeleton**.

humus Dark-coloured organic material in **soil** consisting of decomposing plants and animals,

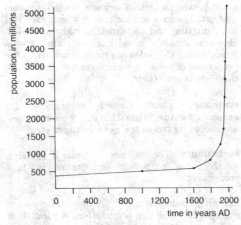

human population curve

and providing nutrients for plants, and ultimately for animals. See **soil**.

hybrid A plant or animal produced as a result of a cross between two parents of the same **species** that are genetically unlike each other, or between two differing but related species.

hydrolysis The breakdown of complex **organic compounds** by **enzyme** action involving the addition of **water**. Hydrolysis is the basic reaction of virtually all processes of **digestion** of **proteins, fats, polysaccharides** and many other compounds.

large
complex compound $+ H_2O$ $\xrightarrow{\text{enzyme}}$ small subunits
(starch)   **(gluose)**

hydrolysis Starch is hydrolysed to glucose.

hydrotropism Tropism relative to water. Plant **roots** are positively hydrotropic, i.e., they grow towards water.

hypertonic Describing a **solution** whose **solute** concentration is higher than the medium on the other side of a **selectively permeable membrane**. Such a solution will gain water by **osmosis**. See **hypotonic, isotonic**. See diagram on page 134.

hypothesis A suggested solution to a scientific problem which must be tested by experimentation and, if not validated, must then be discarded. See **scientific method**.

hypotonic Describing a **solution** whose **solute** concentration is lower than the medium on the

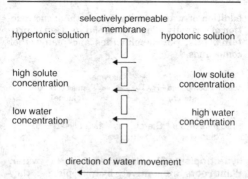

selectively permeable membrane

hypertonic solution   hypotonic solution

high solute concentration   ←   low solute concentration

low water concentration   ←   high water concentration

direction of water movement
←

hypertonic

other side of a selectively permeable membrane. Such a solution will lose water by **osmosis**. See **hypertonic, isotonic**.

ileum The final region of the mammalian **small intestine** which receives food from the **duodenum**. The lining of the ileum secretes **enzymes** which complete the **digestion** of **protein, carbohydrate** and **fat**, into **amino acids**, simple sugars (mainly **glucose**), fatty acids, and glycerol.

Absorption of food occurs in the ileum which has a large absorbing surface due to the presence of thousands of finger-like structures called **villi**. The lining of each villus is very thin, allowing the passage of soluble foods, and each contains a network of **blood capillaries**.

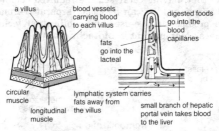

a villus

blood vessels carrying blood to each villus

digested foods go into the blood capillaries

fats go into the lacteal

circular muscle

longitudinal muscle

lymphatic system carries fats away from the villus

small branch of hepatic portal vein takes blood to the liver

ileum A section through the ileum wall (left) and a section of a villus (right).

Amino acid and glucose particles diffuse into the blood capillaries from where they are transported first to the **liver** and then to the general circulation. Fatty acid and glycerol particles pass into the **lacteals** and are circulated via the **lymphatic system**.

Material not absorbed, for example, **roughage**, is passed into the **large intestine**. See **digestion, assimilation**.

imago An adult, sexually mature insect. See **metamorphosis**.

immobilization The process whereby the movement of **cells** or **enzymes** is restricted by attachment to another substance. For example, enzymes can be fixed onto glass beads in such a way that, having catalysed the required chemical reaction, they can be easily separated from the product and re-used. Immobilization techniques are important in **biotechnology**.

glass bead + enzymes → immobilized enzymes on bead

immobilization

immunization Prevention of infection by artificially introducing a **pathogen** into the body. This stimulates **antibody** production and causes immunity to the pathogen, which in some cases lasts a lifetime. In Britain, children are immunized against polio, diphtheria, tetanus, whooping cough and tuberculosis. Girls are also immunized against German measles, a disease which can harm an unborn child. People going abroad may be immunized against diseases such as yellow fever.

implantation Attachment of a mammalian **embryo** to the **uterus** lining at the start of **preg-**

nancy. In preparation for implantation, the uterus wall becomes thicker with new **cells** and an increased **blood** supply. See **fertilization**.

incisors Chisel-shaped cutting **teeth** at the front of the mouth used for biting off pieces of food. See **dental formula, dentition, carnivore, herbivore, omnivore**.

incomplete dominance A genetic condition in which neither of a pair of **alleles** is **dominant** but instead 'blend' to produce an intermediate trait. See **monohybrid inheritance**.

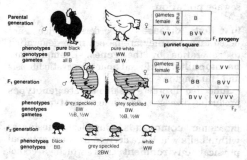

incomplete dominance The inheritance of feather colour in Andalusian fowls.

incubator 1. A heated container used to grow

microorganisms on **nutrient agar plates**. The usual incubation period is 48 hours at 37°C.

2. A heated chamber used to maintain the body temperature of premature babies.

indicator organism An organism which can survive only in certain environmental conditions, and hence one whose presence provides information about the **environment** in which it is found. For example, the **bacterium** *Escherichia coli* lives in animal **gut** and is always present in **faeces**. Although *E. coli* is itself harmless, its presence in water indicates sewage **pollution**.

inherited diseases Disorders which are hereditary, i.e. they are passed from generation to generation by the **genes**. Examples are **haemophilia**; sickle-cell anaemia, cystic fibrosis and Huntington's chorea.

Inherited disorders are due to rare **genotypes** producing disease-susceptible **phenotypes**.

inorganic compounds Chemical substances within **cells** which are derived from the external physical **environment**, and which are not organic. The most abundant cell inorganic compound is water which is present in amounts ranging from 5 to 90%.

The other inorganic components of cells are

mineral salts present in amounts ranging from 1 to 5%. See **organic compounds**.

insulin A vertebrate **hormone** secreted by the Islets of Langerhans in the **pancreas**. Insulin regulates the conversion of **glucose** to **glycogen** in the **liver**. If the concentration of **blood** glucose is high, the rate of secretion of insulin is high, and thus glucose is rapidly converted to liver glycogen. If the concentration of blood glucose is low, less insulin is secreted, an example of feedback regulation found in relation to many hormones. People who suffer from diabetes produce insufficient insulin to control the delicate glucose level balance in their bodies.

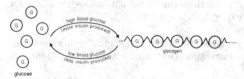

insulin Feedback regulation of insulin secretion.

integrated control The control of **pests** using a combination of chemical and **biological control**.

integument 1. The external protective covering of an animal, e.g. **skin, cuticle**.

2. The protective layer around flowering plant **ovules** which after fertilization forms the **testa**.

intercostal muscles Muscles, positioned between the ribs of mammals, important in **lung** ventilation. See **breathing**.

intestine The region of the **alimentary canal** between the **stomach** and the **anus** or **cloaca**. In vertebrates it is the major area of **digestion** and **absorption** of food, and is usually differentiated into an anterior **small intestine** and a posterior **large intestine**. See **digestion**.

in vitro Describing biological experiments or observations conducted outside an organism, for example in a test tube.

in vivo Describing biological experiments or observations conducted within living organisms.

involuntary (smooth) muscles Muscles associated with internal **tissues** and **organs** in mammals, for example, the **gut** and **blood vessels**, and so-called because they are not directly controlled by the will of the organism. Involuntary muscle actions include contraction and dilation of the **pupil** in the eye, and **peristalsis**. See **voluntary muscles, antagonistic muscles**.

ion An electrically charged **atom** or group of atoms.

iris The structure in the vertebrate **eye** which controls the size of the **pupil** and hence the amount of light entering the **eye**.

irritability See **sensitivity**.

isotonic Describing a **solution** whose **solute** concentration is equal to that of the medium on the other side of a **selectively permeable membrane**. There is no water movement across the membrane by **osmosis** See **hypertonic**, **hypotonic**.

joint The point in a **skeleton** where two or more **bones** meet and movement may be poss-

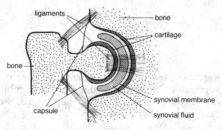

joint Ball and socket joint.

ible. Moveable joints in mammals are of three types:

(a) Ball and socket joints allow movement in several planes.

(b) Hinge joints allow movement in only one plane.

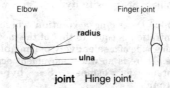

joint   Hinge joint.

(c) Gliding joints occur when two flat surfaces glide over one another, allowing a small amount of movement only.

joint   Gliding joint.

keratin   Strong, fibrous **protein** present in vertebrate **epidermis** forming the outer protective layer of **skin** and also hair, nails, wool, feathers, and horns.

key   A device for identifying unfamiliar organ-

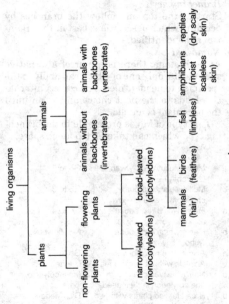

key

isms. The two types of key shown can be used to identify the major divisions of living organisms.

(a) *Branching key*

Start at the top and follow the branches by deciding which descriptions best fit the organism to be identified.

(b) *Numbered key*

At each stage, there is a pair of alternative statements, only one of which can apply to the specimen to be identified. The correct alternative leads to the next choice and so on until the organism is named.

This type of key is preferable to the branching type which can take up too much space.

1 a	Multicellular, usually with chlorophyll	Go to 2
b	Multicellular, without chlorophyll, able to move	Go to 3
2 a	Plants which reproduce using flowers	Go to 4
b	Plants which reproduce without flowers	Non-flowering plants
3 a	Animals with backbones	Go to 5
b	Animals without backbones	Invertebrates
4 a	Narrow-leaved plants with one cotyledon in their seeds	Monocotyledons
b	Broad-leaved plants with two cotyledons in their seeds	Dicotyledons
5 a	Hair present	Mammals
b	Hair absent	Go to 6

6 a	Feathers present	Birds
b	Feathers absent	Go to 7
7 a	Dry, scaly skin	Reptiles
b	Other type of skin	Go to 8
8 a	Four limbs, moist scaleless skin	Amphibians
b	Limbless	Fish

Using the above key, it is now possible to do a simple classification of organisms such as ape, pike, newt, oak, snake, grass and earthworm.

kidney The organ of excretion and osmoregulation in vertebrates, consisting of units called **nephrons**. In humans, the kidneys are a pair of red-brown oval structures at the back of the **abdomen**.

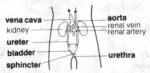

kidney The position of the kidneys and associated organs.

Oxygenated **blood** enters each kidney via the renal **artery**, and the renal **vein** removes deoxygenated blood. Another tube, the **ureter**, connects each kidney with the **bladder**.

The renal artery divides into numerous **arterioles** which terminate in tiny knots of blood

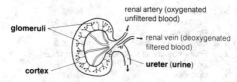

kidney Section through a kidney.

capillaries called **glomeruli**. Each glomerulus (about one million in a human kidney) is enclosed in a cup-shaped organ called a **Bowman's capsule**.

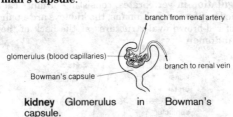

kidney Glomerulus in Bowman's capsule.

Two processes occur in the kidneys:
(a) *Ultrafiltration*. The vessel leaving each glomerulus is narrower than the vessel entering, causing the blood in the glomerulus to be under high pressure, which forces the blood components with smaller molecules through the **selectively permeable** capillary wall into Bowman's capsule.

Large particles (unfiltered)	Small particles (filtered)
Blood cells	Glucose
Plasma proteins	Urea
	Mineral salts
	Water
	Amino acids

(b) *Reabsorption.* The fluid filtered from the blood (filtrate) passes from Bowman's capsule down the renal tubule where reabsorption of useful materials occurs, i.e. all the glucose and amino acids, and some of the salts and water are reabsorbed into the blood.

The liquid remaining after filtration and

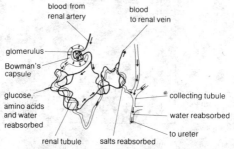

kidney Reabsorption of useful substances.

reabsorption by the kidney is a solution of salts and urea in water (**urine**) and is passed to the **bladder** via the ureters from where it is expelled via the **urethra** under the control of a **sphincter muscle**. See **antidiuretic hormone**.

kidney machine An artificial **kidney** which purifies the **blood** of a person with diseased kidneys. Blood is taken from the person's arm **artery** and passed through a **selectively permeable membrane** where **urea** and excess **mineral salts** are removed into a rinsing solution.

The purified blood is then returned to the person's arm **vein**.

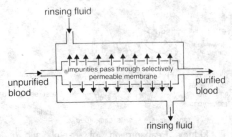

kidney machine

kilojoule The unit used to measure the **energy** content of food. See **food calorimeter**.

kingdom Any of the three great divisions of living organisms, i.e. Animal, Plant, and Protista kingdoms. See **classification**.

lacteals **Lymph** vessels within the **villi** of the vertebrate **intestines**. The products of **fat digestion** (**fatty acids** and **glycerol**) diffuse into the lacteals and are circulated via the **lymphatic system**.

lactic acid An organic acid (CH_3 CH OH COOH) produced during **respiration** in many animal **cells**, including vertebrate **muscle** cells, and certain **bacteria**. See **oxygen debt**.

large intestine The posterior region of the vertebrate **intestine**. In humans, at the entry to the large intestine there is a region called the **caecum**, from which projects the **appendix**, but most of the large intestine consists of the **colon** which leads to the **rectum**. The large intestine receives undigested material from the **ileum**. See **digestion**.

larva An intermediate, sexually immature stage in the **life history** of some animals between hatching from the egg and becoming adult, for example, amphibian tadpoles and butterfly caterpillars. See **metamorphosis**.

larynx A region at the upper end of the **trachea** of tetrapods opening into the **pharynx** and specialized to close the **glottis** during swallowing.

In mammals, amphibians, and reptiles, vocal cords within the larynx produce sound. See **breathing in mammals**.

leaching In **soil**, the washing downwards of **mineral salts** by **water**, mainly rain.

leaf That part of a flowering plant which grows from the **stem** and is typically flat and green.

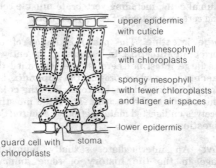

leaf Structure of a dicotyledon leaf.

The functions of leaves are (a) **photosynthesis**, (b) **gas exchange**, and (c) **transpiration**.

lens A transparent structure behind the **pupil** of the vertebrate **eye**, important in focusing the image on the **retina**, and in **accommodation**.

lenticel One of many pores developing in woody **stems** and **roots** when **epidermis** is replaced by bark, through which **gas exchange** occurs. See **gas exchange (plants)**.

leucocyte See **white blood cell**.

lichen A plant formed by **mutualism** between an **alga** and a **fungus**. The alga supplies **carbohydrate** and oxygen to the fungus, and receives **water** and **mineral salts** in return.

life cycle See **life history**.

life history or **life cycle** The various stages of development which organisms undergo from egg to adult. See **alternation of generations**, **metamorphosis**.

ligament A strong band of **collagen** connecting the **bones** at moveable vertebrate **joints**. Ligaments strengthen the joint, allowing movement in only certain directions and preventing dislocation.

lignin An **organic compound** deposited in the cell walls of **xylem** vessels, giving strength. Lignin is an important constituent of wood.

limiting factor Any factor of the **environment** whose level at a particular time inhibits some activity of an organism or **population** of organisms.

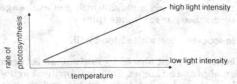

limiting factor Photosynthesis is limited by low light intensity even if temperature increases.

Increasing temperature has little effect at low light intensities. Thus, in this case, light intensity must be the limiting factor.

lipase An **enzyme** which digests **fat** into **fatty acids** and glycerol by **hydrolysis**. In mammals, lipase is secreted by the **pancreas** and the **ileum**. See diagram opposite.

lipid See **fat**.

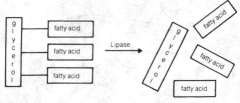

lipase   Hydrolytic breakdown of fat.

liver   The largest organ of the vertebrate body, occupying much of the upper part of the **abdomen**, in close association with the **alimentary canal**. See **digestion**, **circulatory systems**.

Some of the many functions of the liver are:
(a) Production of **bile**;
(b) **Deamination** of excess **amino acids**;
(c) Regulation of **blood** sugar by interconversion of **glucose** and **glycogen**;
(d) Storage of iron, and **vitamins** A and D;
(e) Detoxication of poisonous by-products;
(f) Release and distribution of heat produced by the chemical activity of liver cells;
(g) Conversion of stored **fat** for use by the **tissues**;
(h) Manufacture of **fibrinogen**.

long sight or **hypermetropia**   A human **eye** defect mainly caused by the distance from **lens** to

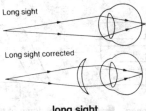

Long sight

Long sight corrected

long sight

retina being shorter than normal. This results in near objects being focused behind the retina giving blurred vision. Long sight is corrected by wearing *converging* (*convex*) lenses.

lungs Breathing **organs** of mammals, amphibians, reptiles, and birds. In mammals, the lungs are two elastic sacs in the **thorax** which can be expanded or compressed by movements of the thorax in such a way that air is continually taken in and expelled. The **trachea** (windpipe) connects the lungs with the atmosphere. It divides into two **bronchi** which enter the lungs and further divide into many smaller *bronchioles* which terminate into millions of air-sacs called **alveoli** which are the **gas exchange** surface and which are in close contact with **blood vessels** bringing blood from and to the **heart**. See **breathing in mammals**, **gas exchange**.

trachea
rings of **cartilage**
bronchus
bronchioles

lungs Air passages in the lung.

luteinizing hormone (LH) A **hormone** secreted by the vertebrate **pituitary gland**. See **ovulation**.

lymph Fluid drained from **blood capillaries** in vertebrates as a result of high pressure at the arterial end of the capillary bed. Lymph or *tissue fluid* which is similar to **plasma** (except for a much lower concentration of **plasma proteins**) bathes the **tissues** and acts as a medium in

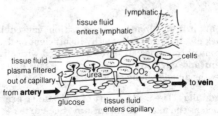

tissue fluid enters lymphatic
lymphatic
tissue fluid
plasma filtered out of capillary
from **artery**
urea
CO_2
O_2
cells
to **vein**
glucose
tissue fluid enters capillary

lymph The lymphatics, capillaries and cells.

which substances are exchanged between capillaries and **cells**. For example, oxygen and **glucose** diffuse into the cells while carbon dioxide and **urea** are removed. Lymph drains back into capillaries or into vessels called lymphatics which then connect with the general circulation via the **lymphatic system**.

lymphatic system   A system of fluid-containing vessels (lymphatics) in vertebrates, which return **lymph** to the general **blood** circulation. The lymphatic system is also important in:
(a) Transporting the products of **fat digestion**;
(b) Production of **white blood cells** and **antibodies**.

lymph nodes   Structures within the **lymphatic system** which filter **bacteria** from **lymph** and produce **white blood cells** and **antibodies**.

malnutrition   Inadequate nutrition caused by lack of a **balanced diet** or by insufficient food. In tropical countries, diseases associated with **protein** and **carbohydrate** deficiency cause many deaths among young children.

medulla   The central part of a **tissue** or **organ** such as the mammalian **kidney**. See **cortex**.

medulla oblongata   The posterior region of the

vertebrate **brain** which is continuous with the **spinal cord** and which in mammals controls **heartbeat**, **breathing**, **peristalsis** and other involuntary actions.

meiosis A method of *nuclear division* that occurs during the formation of **gametes** when a **diploid** nucleus gives rise to four **haploid** nuclei. There are two consecutive divisions in the process, as shown below.

During the first division of meiosis the homologous chromosomes may exchange genetic material as they lie side-by-side, and this leads to variation in the resulting nuclei. This process is called *crossing over*.

First division

Interphase
contents of nucleus
indistinct

Prophase
contents of nucleus
become clear

Homologous chromosomes
form pair. Nuclear membrane
breaks down

each chromosome
can be seen to consist
of two chromatids
joined by a centromere

Metaphase
nuclear spindle
forms and chromosomes
move to the equator

Anaphase
centromeres repel
each other carrying
chromosomes towards
the poles of the spindle

Telophase
nuclear membranes
form around the
groups of chromosomes

Second division

Metaphase
Nuclear spindles form
and chromosomes move
to the equator

Anaphase
Centromeres divide
and repel each other
carrying chromatids
towards the poles

Telophase
Nuclear spindles break
down and membranes
form around haploid
groups of chromosomes

meiosis Stages in the two divisions of the process.

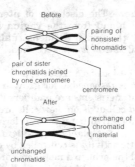

meiosis Crossing over between non-sister chromatids.

menopause The time at the end of the reproductive period of human females when **menstrual cycles** cease to occur.

menstrual cycle The reproductive cycle occurring in female primates (monkeys, apes, humans). This cycle is under the control of **hormones**. In human females, the cycle lasts about 28 days, during which the **uterus** is prepared for **implantation**. If **fertilization** does not occur, the new uterus lining and unfertilized **ovum** are expelled, which results in bleeding from the **vagina (menstruation)**. See **ovulation**.

menstruation The discharge of **uterus** lining **tissue** and **blood** from the **vagina** in human females at the end of a **menstrual cycle** in which **fertilization** has not occurred.

meristem A localized **tissue** of active **cell division** which is responsible for **growth** in plants. The **cells** at meristems are undifferentiated, but by repeated cell division, new cells are produced which ultimately differentiate to form the specialized tissues of plants, e.g. **xylem**, **phloem**. Meristematic activity is controlled by plant **hormones** and the principal meristems are **root tip**, **shoot** tip and **cambium**. See **cell differentiation**, **primary growth**, **secondary growth**.

messenger RNA See **RNA**, **protein synthesis**.

metabolic water One of the products of aerobic **respiration** which is an important source of water for desert animals.

metabolism The sum of all the physical and chemical processes occurring within a living organism. These include both the synthesis (*anabolism*) and breakdown (*catabolism*) of compounds. See **basal metabolic rate**.

metamorphosis The period in the **life history**

metabolism The synthesis and breakdown of compounds within an organism.

of some animals when the juvenile stage is transformed into an adult.

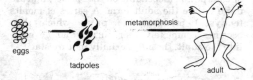

metamorphosis Amphibians go through a tadpole stage.

Incomplete metamorphosis is a type of development in which there are relatively few changes from juvenile form to adult. It occurs in insects such as the dragonfly, locust and cockroach, in which the juvenile form (**nymph**) resembles the adult except that it is smaller, wingless, and sexually immature.

Complete metamorphosis involves great changes from **larva** to adult. It occurs in insects

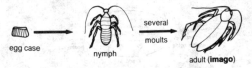

egg case   nymph   several moults   adult (**imago**)

metamorphosis Incomplete metamorphosis in the cockroach.

such as butterfly, moth, housefly, etc., and the larvae in such life histories are maggots, grubs, or caterpillars (depending on the species) and are quite unlike the adult form. A series of moults (**ecdyses**) produces the **pupa** which then becomes completely reorganized and develops into the adult, the only sexually mature stage.

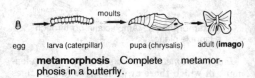

egg   larva (caterpillar)   moults   pupa (chrysalis)   adult (**imago**)

metamorphosis Complete metamorphosis in a butterfly.

microbe An alternative term for **microorganism**.

microbiology The study of **microorganisms**.

microbiology experiments The use of sterile **nutrient agar plates** to culture **microorgan-**

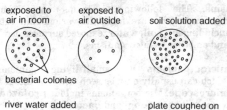

exposed to air in room

exposed to air outside

soil solution added

bacterial colonies

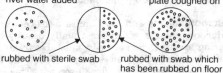

river water added

plate coughed on

rubbed with sterile swab

rubbed with swab which has been rubbed on floor

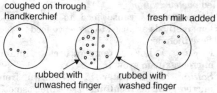

coughed on through handkerchief

fresh milk added

rubbed with unwashed finger

rubbed with washed finger

sour milk added   fresh cheese   stale cheese

moulds

microbiology experiments

isms. The following diagrams show that microorganisms are found in various habitats including air, **soil, water**, exposed surfaces, food, and on other living organisms.

microorganisms Very small living organisms which can usually only be seen with the aid of a **microscope**. Microorganisms include **protozoa, algae, viruses, fungi** and **bacteria**.

microorganisms and food Most foods contain **microorganisms** which are usually destroyed during cooking. Some foods must be treated before consumption, an example being milk, which is heated at 80°C for 30 seconds. This is called *pasteurization*.

Microorganisms cause food to go off, and various methods are used to preserve food.

These include:

(a) *Freezing* Low temperatures inhibit microorganism growth;

(b) *Salting* causes water to be drawn from microorganisms resulting in so-called osmotic death;

(c) *Dehydration* of food deprives microorganisms of necessary water.

(d) *Smoking* food adds chemicals which kill microorganisms;

(e) *High temperature sterilization* is used in some canned foods.

(f) *Chemical preservatives*, which cause an unfavourable acid **pH**, are added to some foods, e.g. acetic acid (vinegar).

micropyle 1. A pore in a **seed** through which water is absorbed at the start of **germination**.
2. Pore in the **ovule** of a **flower** through which the **pollen** tube delivers the male **gamete**.
3. Pore in the **ovum** of insects through which the **spermatozoon** enters.

microscope An instrument used to magnify structures, for example, **cells** or organisms, which are not visible to the naked eye.
(a) *The light microscope* Light illuminates the specimen which is magnified by glass lenses.

The magnification of the microscope is found by multiplying the magnification of the objective lens (e.g. ×40) by the magnification of the eyepiece lens (e.g. ×10) to give the total

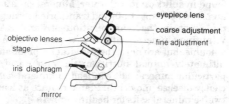

microscope   Parts of a light microscope

magnification (in this example ×400). The maximum possible magnification using a light microscope is ×1500. Thin specimens are placed on a glass slide and may be stained with dyes which show up particular structures.

(b) *The phase-contrast microscope* allows the viewing of transparent and unstained structures.

(c) *The electron microscope* is the most advanced type, giving magnification as high as ×500 000.

milk teeth or **deciduous teeth**   The first set of **teeth** occurring in most mammals. For example, humans have 20 milk teeth which are replaced during childhood by the larger permanent teeth.

mineral salts   Components of **soil** formed from rock weathering and **humus** *mineralization* and found in **solution** in soil water. Mineral salts are absorbed by plant **roots** and transported through the plant in the **transpiration stream**. Like **vitamins**, mineral salts are required in tiny amounts, but are nevertheless vital for plant and ultimately animal nutrition; the absence of a particular mineral salt can lead to mineral deficiency disease and death. Plants require at least twelve mineral salts for healthy growth.

(a) *Essential elements* required in relatively

large quantities: nitrogen, phosphorus, sulphur, potassium, calcium, magnesium.

(b) *Trace elements* required in very small amounts: manganese, copper, zinc, iron, boron, molybdenum.

Some mineral salts are required by plants, some are required by animals, and some by both.

Mineral salt	Function	Some effects of deficiency
Phosphorus	Components of ATP, nucleic acids, cell membrane, animal bones.	Stunted plant growth.
Calcium	Component of plant cell walls and animal bones.	Rickets in humans.
Nitrogen	Component of protein and nucleic acids.	Poor reproductive development in plants.
Iron	Component of haemoglobin.	Anaemia in humans.
Magnesium	Component of chlorophyll.	Pale yellow plant leaves (chlorosis).

mineral salts Some important minerals and their functions.

mitochondrion A microscopic **cell organelle**

in the **cytoplasm** of aerobic cells, in which some **respiration** reactions occur. The inner membrane of a mitochondrion wall is highly folded, giving rise to a series of partitions called *cristae*, which greatly increase the surface area for the attachment of respiratory enzymes.
See **aerobe, enzymes**.

cristae

1 μ

mitochondrion   Section showing cristae.

mitosis   The process necessary for the growth of an organism, by which the **nucleus** of a **cell** divides in such a way that the resultant *daughter cells* receive precisely the same numbers and types of **chromosomes** as the original *mother cell*. During this type of nuclear division the chromosomes of the mother cell (the dividing cell) are first duplicated and then passed in identical sets to the two daughter cells.

In stage 1, Chromosomes appear as coiled threads. Two structures called *centrioles* are seen outside the nucleus.

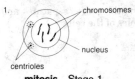

mitosis Stage 1.

Each chromosome makes a duplicate of itself. These duplicates or *chromatids* are joined at a *centromere*.

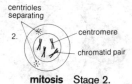

mitosis Stage 2.

The *nuclear membrane* disappears. The centrioles move to opposite poles of the cell and produce a system of fibres called a *spindle*. The chromatid pairs line up at the equator of the cell.

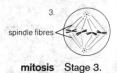

mitosis Stage 3.

The chromatid pairs separate and move to opposite poles of the cell.

mitosis   Stage 4.

New nuclear membranes form and the **cytoplasm** starts to divide.

mitosis   Stage 5.

The chromosomes disappear and the cells return to the resting state.

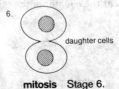

mitosis   Stage 6.

molars Together with **premolars** these **teeth** are also known as **cheek teeth**. They are broad crowned grinding teeth at the sides and back of the mouth, used for crushing food prior to swallowing. Found in **omnivores** and **herbivores** they are replaced by **carnassial** teeth in **carnivores**. See **dental formula, dentition**.

molecule The smallest complete part of a chemical **compound** that can take part in a reaction. Within a molecule **atoms** occur in fixed proportions.

monocotyledons The smaller of the two subsets of flowering plants, the other being **dicotyledons**. The characteristics of monocotyledons are:
(a) One **cotyledon** in the **seed**;
(b) Parallel **veins** in **leaves**;
(c) Narrow leaves;
(d) Scattered **vascular bundles** in **stem**;
(e) **Flower** parts usually in threes or in multiples of threes.
Examples are cereals and grasses.

monohybrid inheritance The inheritance of one pair of contrasting characteristics.

For example, in the fruit-fly *Drosophila*, one variety is **purebreeding** normal-winged, and another is pure-breeding vestigial-winged, the normal-winged **allele** being **dominant** to the

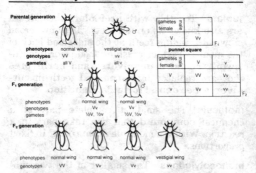

Parental generation

phenotypes	normal wing	vestigial wing
genotypes	VV	vv
gametes	all V	all v

gametes female	male	v
	V	Vv

F₁

punnet square

gametes female	male V	v
V	VV	Vv
v	Vv	vv

F₂

F₁ generation

phenotypes	normal wing	normal wing
genotypes	Vv	Vv
gametes	½V, ½v	½V, ½v

F₂ generation

phenotypes	normal wing	normal wing	normal wing	vestigial wing
genotypes	VV	Vv	Vv	vv

monohybrid inheritance The result of crossing normal-winged female *Drosophila* with vestigial-winged males.

vestigial-winged allele.

Approximate ratio in F_2 generation:

$$\frac{\text{normal}}{\text{vestigial wing}} = \frac{3}{1}$$

When normal-winged is crossed with vestigial-winged, the vestigial trait seems to disappear, only to reappear again to a limited extent in the next generation, suggesting that the **F₁ generation** must have possessed this trait without showing it. A trait such as normal wing which always appears in a cross between contrasting parents is described as **dominant**, while a trait such as vestigial wing which is 'lost' in F_1 generation **progeny**, apparently masked by a dominant trait, is called **recessive**.

For each trait, an organism receives one **gene** from the male **gamete** and one from the female gamete, i.e., the **zygote**, and the resulting organism contains two genes for every trait, but the gametes contain only one (as a result of **meiosis**). If the paired genes for a particular trait are identical, the organism is said to be **homozygous** or **pure** for that trait. When an organism has two different genes for a trait, it is described as **heterozygous** or **hybrid**. Alternative forms of a gene are described as *allelomorphs* or alleles. Hence, if the allele for normal wing is represented by V and that for vestigial wing by v:

> VV is homozygous normal wing
> Vv is heterozygous normal wing
> vv is homozygous vestigial wing

Organisms, homozygous for a particular trait, produce only one type of gamete for that trait, while heterozygous organisms produce two gamete types. The results of **fertilization** can then be worked out using a **punnet square**. See **backcross, incomplete dominance**.

monosaccharides Single **sugar carbohydrates** which are the subunits of more complex carbohydrates, and named on the basis of the number of carbon atoms present. For example:

$C_3H_6O_3$ $C_5H_{10}O_5$ $C_6H_{12}O_6$
triose sugar   pentose sugar   hexose sugar

Hexose sugars are common carbohydrates and include **glucose**.

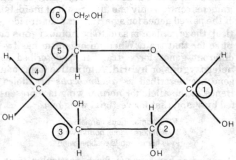

monosaccharides Structure of glucose ($C_6H_{12}O_6$).

motile Describes organisms or parts of organisms that can move.

mucus A slimy fluid secreted by **goblet cells** in vertebrate **epithelia**. Mucus traps dust and **bacteria** in mammalian air passages, lubricates the surfaces of internal organs, and facilitates the movement of food through the **gut** while preventing the digestive enzymes from reaching and digesting the gut itself.

multicellular (of an **organism**) Consisting of many **cells**. Most animals and plants are multicellular. Compare **unicellular**.

muscle Animal **tissue** consisting of **cells** which are capable of contraction as a result of **nerve impulses**, thus producing movement, both of the organism as a whole and of internal **organs**. See **antagonistic muscles**, **involuntary muscles**, **voluntary muscles**.

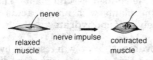

relaxed muscle · nerve · nerve impulse · contracted muscle

muscle Contraction.

mutagenic agents Factors which speed up the rate of **mutation**. These include certain chemicals, e.g. *mustard gas* and *irradiation* with *ultraviolet rays*, *X-rays* and *atomic radiation*.

mutation A change in the structure of **DNA** in **chromosomes**. Mutations occur rarely; when they occur in the **gametes**, or the cells that give rise to them, they are inheritable and most confer disadvantages on the organisms inheriting them. Mutations can result in beneficial **variations** within a **population** which can lead to **evolution**, and although they occur naturally, they can also be induced by exposure to excessive radiation or other **mutagenic agents**.

mutualism A **symbiotic** relationship in which both organisms benefit. For example, the **intestinal bacteria** of **herbivores** digest the **cellulose** of plant **cell** walls, the products of which are then used by the herbivore.

mycorrhiza A **symbiotic** association between **fungi** and the **roots** of certain plants. The fungi provides the plants with **amino acids** and in return receives **carbohydrates**.

nastic movement A growth response by plants to a stimulus that is independent of the direction of the stimulus. For example, the opening and closing of a flower in response to light intensity. See **tropism**.

natural selection The theory proposed by Charles Darwin to explain how **evolution** could have taken place. Darwin suggested that individuals in a **species** differ in the extent to which they are adapted to their **environment**. Thus, in **competition** for food, etc., the better

adapted organisms will survive, and pass on
their favourable **variations**, while the less well
adapted will be eliminated.

nephron A subunit of the vertebrate **kidney**,
consisting of a **Bowman's capsule**,
glomerulus, and *renal tubule*. See **excretion**,
osmoregulation.

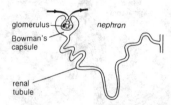

glomerulus

Bowman's
capsule

nephron

renal
tubule

nephron   Section through a nephron.

nerve impulses The electrical messages by
which information is transmitted rapidly
throughout **nervous systems**. Nerve impulses
are initiated at **receptor cells** as a result of
stimuli from the **environment**. In vertebrates,
the impulses are conducted to the **central
nervous system**, where they trigger other
impulses which are relayed to **effector organs**.
See **neurones, synapse**.

nervous system A network of specialized **cells**

in **multicellular** animals, which acts as a link between **receptors** and **effectors**, and thus coordinates the animal's activities. In mammals, the nervous system consists of the **brain** and **spinal cord** (which together form the **central nervous system**) and **neurones** connecting all parts of the body.

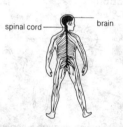

spinal cord ——— brain

nervous system The main parts of the human nervous system.

neural Describes functions and parts of the body related to the **nervous system**.

neurones (or **nerve cells**) Cells which are the basic units of mammalian **nervous systems**. There are two types of nerve cells:

(a) *Sensory neurones* Conduct **nerve impulses** from **receptors** to the **central nervous system** (CNS), i.e. from **eyes**, **ears**, **skin**, etc.;

(b) *Motor neurones*. Conduct **nerve impulses**

from the CNS to **effectors**, such as **muscles** and **endocrine glands**.

Each nerve cell consists of three parts:

(a) A *cell body* containing **cytoplasm** and **nucleus** and forming the *grey matter* in the **brain** and **spinal cord**;

(b) Fibres which carry nerve impulses into cell bodies. In sensory neurones, this fibre is a single *dendron* while in motor neurones there are numerous *dendrites*. In the CNS such fibres form *white matter*;

(c) Fibres called **axons** which carry nerve impulses from cell bodies.

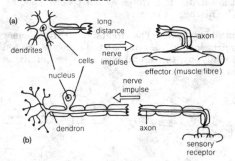

neurones The structure of (a) motor neurone and (b) sensory neurone.

neutralize See **alkali**.

neutron   See **atom**.

niche   The status or way of life of an organism within a **community**. For example, a **herbivore** and a **carnivore** may share the same **habitat** but their different feeding methods mean that they occupy different niches.

nitrification   The conversion of **organic** nitrogen compounds by nitrifying **bacteria** in the **soil**, for example, ammonia into nitrates which can be absorbed by plants. Ammonia is first converted to nitrites by *Nitrosomonas* **bacteria** and the nitrites to nitrates by *Nitrobacter* **species**. See **nitrogen cycle**.

nitrogen cycle   The circulation of the element nitrogen and its compounds in nature, caused mainly by the **metabolic** processes of living organisms.

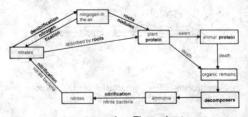

nitrogen cycle   The main steps.

nitrogen fixation The conversion of atmospheric nitrogen by certain **microorganisms** into **organic** nitrogen compounds. Nitrogen-fixing **bacteria** live either in **soil**, air, or within the **root nodules**, of leguminous plants. The activity of these organisms, such as *Azotobacter* and *Rhizobium*, enriches the soil with nitrogen compounds. See **nitrogen cycle, root nodule**.

normal distribution curve A bell-shaped curve obtained when *continuous variation* is measured in a **population**. See **variation**.

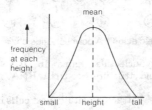

normal distribution curve

nuclear division See **meiosis, mitosis**.

nucleic acids **Organic compounds** found in all living organisms, particularly associated with the **nucleus** of the **cell**, and consisting of subunits called *nucleotides*.

The sugar group of one nucleotide can combine

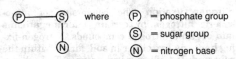

where   (P) = phosphate group

(S) = sugar group

(N) = nitrogen base

nucleic acids Structure of a single nucleotide.

with the phosphate group of another to form a *polynucleotide* chain.

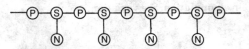

nucleic acids A polynucleotide chain.

Such polynucleotide chains are the basis of nucleic acid structure. See **DNA**, **RNA**.

nucleus A structure within most **cells** in which the **chromosomes** are located. It is isolated from

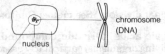

nucleus The nucleus of a cell and one of its chromosomes.

the **cytoplasm** by a *nuclear membrane*, and chromosomes are visible only during nuclear division. As the chromosomes contain the hereditary information, the nucleus controls all the cell's activities through the action of the genetic material **DNA**.

nutrient agar plate See **agar**.

nymph The juvenile form of certain insects which resembles the **imago** except that it is smaller, wingless and sexually immature. See **metamorphosis**.

oesophagus A region of the **alimentary canal**, connecting the mouth with the digestive areas. In vertebrates, it runs between the **pharynx** and the **stomach** and transports food by **peristalsis**. See **digestion**.

oestrogen A **hormone** secreted by vertebrate **ovaries** which stimulates the development of **secondary sexual characteristics** in female mammals and is important in the **menstrual cycle**.

olfactory Describes parts of the body and functions related to the sense of **smell**.

omnivore An animal which feeds on both

plants and animals. Omnivores include man whose **dentition**, like other omnivores, contains both **herbivore** and **carnivore** features, consisting of biting, ripping and grinding teeth, which suit the mixed diet. See **dental formula**, **teeth**.

optic Describes parts of the body related to the **eye** and its functions.

optic nerve A **cranial nerve** of vertebrates conducting **nerve impulses** from the **retina** of the **eye** to the **brain**.

oral Describes parts of the body and functions related to the mouth.

oral hygiene The maintenance of healthy conditions in the human mouth in order to reduce tooth decay. **Bacteria** in the mouth convert food particles stuck to **teeth** into **acid** which attacks the teeth and causes decay. Regular brushing with toothpaste reduces the likelihood of tooth decay.

order Unit used in the **classification** of living organisms, consisting of one or more **families**.

organ A collection of different **tissues** in a plant or animal which form a structural and functional unit. Examples are the **liver** and a plant **leaf**.

Different organs may then be associated together to constitute a *system*, e.g. the digestive system.

cells→tissues→organs→systems

organelle A structure found in the **cytoplasm** of cells, e.g. **mitochondria**, **chloroplasts**. See **cell differentiation**.

organ of corti See **cochlea**.

organic compounds Compounds containing the element carbon, found in all living organisms. The major organic compounds are **carbohydrates**, **fats**, **nucleic acids**, **proteins**, and **vitamins**. See **inorganic compounds**.

osmoregulation Control of the osmotic pressure, and therefore the **water** content, of an organism. See **osmosis**.

In terrestrial organisms, water is gained from food and drink and as a by-product of **respiration**, and is lost by sweating, in exhaled air, and as urine.

Water and mineral salt balance in terrestrial animals is mainly under the control of the **kidneys**. For osmoregulation in fish, see diagram on page 186.

osmosis The **diffusion** of **solvent** (usually

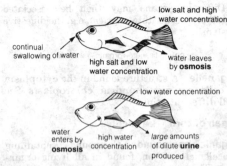

low salt and high
water concentration

continual
swallowing of water

high salt and low
water concentration

water leaves
by **osmosis**

low water concentration

water
enters by
osmosis

high water
concentration

large amounts
of dilute **urine**
produced

osmoregulation Water balance in a seawater fish (above) and a freshwater fish
(below).

water) particles through a **selectively permeable membrane** from a region of high
solvent concentration to a region of lower solvent
concentration.

Examples of selectively permeable membranes
are (a) the **cell membrane**, and (b) visking
(dialysis) tubing. Such membranes are thought
to have tiny pores which allow the rapid passage
of small water particles, but restrict the passage
of larger *solute* particles.

Since the cell membrane is selectively permeable, osmosis is important in the passage of

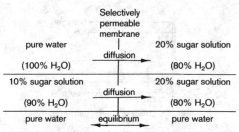

	Selectively permeable membrane	
pure water	diffusion →	20% sugar solution
(100% H$_2$O)		(80% H$_2$O)
10% sugar solution	diffusion →	20% sugar solution
(90% H$_2$O)		(80% H$_2$O)
pure water	← equilibrium	pure water

water into and out of cells and organisms, and depends on **osmotic pressure**. See **turgor, wall pressure**.

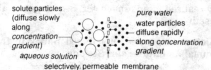

solute particles (diffuse slowly along *concentration gradient*)

aqueous solution

pure water
water particles diffuse rapidly along *concentration gradient*

selectively permeable membrane

osmosis Passage of solvent (water) particles through a selectively permeable membrane.

osmotic pressure The pressure exerted by the osmotic movement of **water** which can be demonstrated in an osmometer.

Water moves into the solution in the visking bag by osmosis, causing the liquid level in the tube to

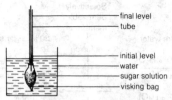

osmotic pressure   An osmometer.

rise. Osmotic pressure depends on the relative **solute** concentrations of the **solutions** involved. The osmotic pressure that a solution is capable of developing is called its *osmotic potential*, but is only realized in an osmometer. See **turgor**, **wall pressure**.

ossicles   The three tiny linked **bones** in the mammalian **middle ear**. See **ear**.

oval window   A membrane separating the **middle ear** and **inner ear** in mammals. See **ear**.

ovary   1. A hollow region in the **carpel** of a **flower**, containing one or more **ovules**. See **fertilization**.
2. The reproductive **organ** of female animals. In vertebrates, there are two ovaries which produce the **ova** and also release certain sex **hormones**. See **fertilization**, **ovulation**.

oviduct A tube in animals which carries **ova** from the **ovaries**. In mammals there are two oviducts leading to the **uterus** and **fertilization** occurs within the **oviduct**. See **fertilization**.

ovulation The release of an **ovum** from a mature **Graafian follicle** on the surface of a vertebrate **ovary**, from where it passes into the **oviduct** and then into the **uterus**.

Ovulation in the human female. Ovulation is controlled by **hormones** from the **pituitary gland** and the sequence of events in the female's reproductive behaviour is called the **menstrual cycle. Follicle stimulating hormone (FSH)**

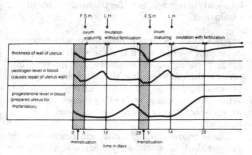

ovulation The main features of the human menstrual cycle.

induces the maturation of **ova** and causes the ovaries to produce **oestrogen**. **Luteinizing hormone (LH)** triggers ovulation and also the release of **progesterone** by the ovaries.

If the mature ovum is not fertilized, it is expelled with the new uterus lining and some **blood** via the **vagina**, a process called **menstruation**.

ovule A structure in flowering plants which develops into a **seed** after **fertilization**. See **carpel**.

ovum An unfertilized female **gamete** produced in the **ovary** of many animals, and containing a **haploid nucleus**. See **fertilization**, **meiosis**, **ovulation**.

oxygen debt A deficit of oxygen which occurs in **aerobes** when work is done with inadequate oxygen supply. For example, in mammalian **muscle** during **exercise**, the oxygen supply may be insufficient to meet the **energy** demand. When this happens, the **cells** produce energy by **anaerobic respiration**, **lactic acid** being a by-product.

The accumulation of lactic acid causes muscle fatigue but is eventually reduced as oxygen intake returns to normal after the period of exercise. This shortfall of oxygen must be repaid by increased oxygen intake (panting). See **blood**, **respiration**.

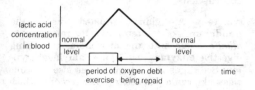

oxygen debt The effect of exercise on the lactic acid concentration of the blood.

ozone layer A layer of the atmospheric gas ozone (O_3) which surrounds planet earth. It is thought that the layer is being depleted as the result of reacting with *chlorofluocarbons* (CFC) which are gases released by aerosol cans. This may allow more *ultraviolet* (UV) radiation from the sun to reach the earth's surface, causing skin cancer and disturbing weather patterns.

pacemaker 1. A structure in the *right atrium* of the **heart**, which initiates the **heartbeat**. 2. An electronic device implanted in the **heart** to stimulate and regulate the **heartbeat**.

palaeontology See **fossil**.

palisade mesophyll The main **tissue** carrying

out **photosynthesis** in the **leaf**, situated below the upper **epidermis**, and containing many **chloroplasts**.

pancreas A gland situated near the **duodenum** of vertebrates. It releases an *alkaline* fluid into the duodenum, containing digestive **enzymes**, e.g. **lipase**, **amylase**, **trypsin**. See **digestion**. The pancreas also contains **tissue** known as the *Islets of Langerhans*, which secretes the **hormone insulin**.

parasite An organism that feeds in or on another living organism which is called the *host*, and which does not benefit and may be harmed by the relationship. Parasites of man include fleas, lice and tapeworms. See **ectoparasite**, **endoparasite**.

parasitism See **symbiosis**.

parental generation The first organisms crossed in a breeding experiment, producing **progeny** known as the F_1 **generation**. See **monohybrid inheritance**.

patella A **bone** over the front of the knee **joint** in many vertebrates. In humans it is the knee-cap. See **endoskeleton**.

pathogen A term used to describe an organism

causing disease in another **species**. Examples are **viruses**, **bacteria** and tapeworms. See **parasite**.

pathogenic   microorganisms Microorganisms which cause disease. Such organisms enter the body by various routes: contaminated food, inhaled air, insect bites, **skin** wounds. However, the body has mechanisms for preventing infection.

(a) The **acid pH** of the **stomach** kills many organisms;
(b) The formation of **blood clots** at wounds restricts entry;
(c) **Phagocytosis** by **white blood cells**;
(d) **Antibodies** in the **blood** neutralize the poisons produced by microorganisms;
(e) The action of **cilia** and **mucus** in the air passages.

If these natural defence mechanisms are overcome, the infection can then be treated using **antibiotics**. Prevention is also possible by **immunization**.

pectoral Describes that part of the body at the **anterior** end of the trunk of an animal (e.g. the shoulders) to which the forelimbs are attached.

pelvic Describes that part of the body of an animal which forms the lower abdomen and to which the hindlimbs are attached.

penicillin The first **antibiotic**, discovered by Alexander Fleming in 1928.

penis An **organ** in mammals by which the male gametes (**spermatozoa**) are introduced into the female body. It also contains the **urethra** through which **urine** is discharged. See **fertilization**.

pentadactyl limb A limb with five digits, characteristic of **tetrapod** animals. There is a basic arrangement of bones that is modified in many species. See **endoskeleton**.

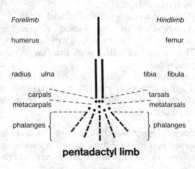

pentadactyl limb

pepsin A **protease enzyme** secreted by the wall of the vertebrate **stomach**, along with hydrochloric acid. The acid provides a suitable

pH for pepsin which digests long protein chains into shorter chains of **amino acids** called **peptides**.

pepsin The action of pepsin on protein.

peptide A compound consisting of two or more **amino acids** linked between the *amino* group of one and the *acid* group of the next. The link between adjacent amino acids is called a *peptide bond*, and when many amino acids are joined in this way, the whole complex is called a *polypeptide*, which is the basis of **protein** structure.

peptide Two amino acids are joined in a peptide bond.

peristalsis Waves of muscular contraction passing along and causing movement of contents in tubular organs, for example, in mammals, the **alimentary canal** and also **ureters** and **oviducts**. Peristalsis is caused by the rhythmic and coordinated contraction and relaxation of **involuntary** circular and longitudinal **muscles**. See **antagonistic muscles**.

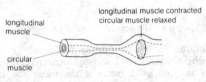

longitudinal muscle contracted
circular muscle relaxed

longitudinal muscle

circular muscle

peristalsis

pest Any living organism which is considered to have a detrimental effect on humans. Methods used to combat pests include:
(a) Spraying with chemicals (**pesticides**);
(b) Using natural **predators** against the pest;
(c) Introducing **parasites** and **pathogens** to the pest **population**;
(d) Introducing sterile individuals to the pest population, thus reducing reproductive capacity.

pesticide A chemical compound, often delivered in a spray, which kills pests or inhibits

Example of pest	Effect on humans
Weeds, locusts	Reduce the growth of plants and crops.
Foot and mouth virus	Causes disease in domestic animals.
Woodworm, wet rot fungus	Damages buildings.
Mosquitoes, lice	Transmit human disease.

pest Some pests and the damage they cause.

their growth.

Examples:

(a) *Herbicides*: weedkillers such as paraquat;
(b) *Fungicides*: seed dressings such as *organo-mercury* compounds;
(c) *Insecticides*: fly sprays used in the home; sprays released from aircraft against locusts. DDT (now banned in Britain) has been used against mosquitoes and lice.

The disadvantages of pesticides are:

(a) They may kill organisms other than the target pest;
(b) The concentration of a pesticide increases as it passes through a **food chain**;
(c) Some decompose slowly and may accumulate

into harmful doses within organisms;
(d) By killing off susceptible organisms, they allow resistant individuals to grow and multiply with reduced **competition**.

pH A measure of the degree of *acidity* or *alkalinity* of a **solution**.

pH The pH scale.

phagocytosis The process by which **cells** (*phagocytes*) surround and engulf a food particle which is then digested. Phagocytosis is the feeding method employed by some **unicellular** protozoans, e.g. *Amoeba*. It is also one of the methods by which **white blood cells** destroy invading **microorganisms**.

phagocytosis The phagocyte engulfs and digests a food particle.

pharynx A region of the vertebrate **alimentary canal** between the **mouth** and the **oesophagus**. In humans it is the back of the nose and throat, and when stimulated by food, swallowing is initiated.

phenotype The physical characteristics of an organism resulting from the influence of **genotype** and **environment**. See **monohybrid inheritance**.

phloem **Tissue** within plants which transports **carbohydrate** from the **leaves** throughout the plant. Phloem consists of tubes which are formed from columns of living **cells** in which the horizontal cross walls have become perforated. This allows carbohydrate to move from one phloem cell into the next and thus through the plant. Because of their structure phloem tubes are also called *sieve tubes*. See **companion cell**, **leaf**, **root**, **secondary growth**, **stem**, **translocation**.

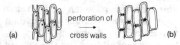

(a)   perforation of   (b)
cross walls

phloem Phloem cells (a) become sieve tubes (b).

photoperiod The length of daylight which is important in many plant and animal **responses**, such as flowering in plants; migration in birds. See **rhythmical behaviour**.

photoreceptor A **sense organ** which is stimulated by light, such as the **eye**.

photosynthesis The process by which green plants make **carbohydrate** from carbon dioxide and **water**. The **energy** for the reaction comes from sunlight which is absorbed by the **chlorophyll** within **chloroplasts**, and oxygen is evolved as a by-product. Overall reaction:

$$\text{carbon} + \text{water} \atop \text{dioxide} \quad \xrightarrow[\text{chlorophyll}]{\text{light energy}} \quad \text{carbohydrate} + \text{oxygen}$$

$$6CO_2 + 6H_2O \quad \xrightarrow{} \quad C_6H_{12}O_6 \; + \; 6O_2$$

Photosynthesis is in fact a two-stage reaction involving:
(a) The light reaction in which light energy is used to split water into *hydrogen* (which passes to the next stage) and *oxygen* (which is released);
(b) The dark reaction in which the hydrogen from the light reaction combines with carbon dioxide to form carbohydrates.

It is the source of all food and the basis of **food chains**, while the release of oxygen replenishes the oxygen content of the atmosphere.

phototropism **Tropism** relative to light. Plant **shoots** are positively phototropic, i.e., they grow towards light.

light from one side →

phototropism

phylum A unit used in the **classification** of living organisms, consisting of one or more **classes**. The term **division** is often substituted in plant classification.

phytoplankton See **plankton**.

pinna A flap of **skin** and **cartilage** at the outside end of the mammalian outer ear. See **ear**.

pitfall trap A trap used to collect organisms living on or just below the **soil** surface and from leaf litter. Examples of organisms caught are beetles and centipedes. See diagram on page 202.

pituitary gland An **endocrine gland** at the base of the vertebrate **brain**. It produces numerous **hormones** including **antidiuretic**

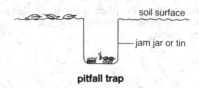

pitfall trap

hormone and **follicle-stimulating hormone**, many of which regulate the activity of other endocrine glands. The pituitary gland's own secretion is in many cases regulated by the brain. See **hormones**.

placenta An **organ** developing during **pregnancy** in the mammalian **uterus** and forming a close association between maternal and foetal **blood** circulations. The placenta allows passage of food and oxygen to the **foetus** and removes carbon dioxide and **urea**.

plankton Microscopic animals (**zooplankton**) and plants (**phytoplankton**) which float in the surface waters of lakes and seas. Plankton are important as the basis of aquatic **food chains**.

plasma The clear fluid of vertebrate **blood** in which the blood **cells** are suspended. It is an aqueous **solution** in which are dissolved many compounds in transit around the body. Examples:

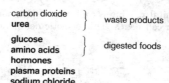

carbon dioxide ⎱
urea ⎰ waste products

glucose ⎱
amino acids ⎰ digested foods
hormones
plasma proteins
sodium chloride

plasma proteins Proteins dissolved in the **plasma** of vertebrate **blood**. Examples are **antibodies**, **fibrinogen**, and some **hormones**.

plasmid A circular length of **genes** found in **bacteria cells**, independent of the bacterial **chromosome**. See **genetic engineering**.

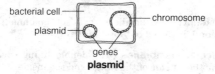

bacterial cell

plasmid

chromosome

genes

plasmid

plasmolysis The loss of **water** from a plant cell by **osmosis** when the cell is surrounded by a **solution** whose water concentration is less than that of the cell **vacuole** (for example, a strong **sugar** or salt solution). **Osmosis** causes water to pass out of the cell, making the vacuole shrink, resulting in the pulling away of the **cytoplasm** from the cell wall.

Plasmolysis can be induced and reversed

experimentally, but continued plasmolysis results in cell death. This osmotic death rarely

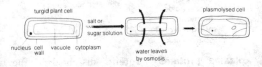

plasmolysis

occurs naturally but can result from adding excess **fertilizer** to plants since this induces plasmolysis, or what is called 'plant burning'.

platelet The smallest **cell** of mammalian **blood**, involved in **blood clotting**.

pleural membranes The double lining covering the outside of the **lungs** and the inside of the **thorax** in mammals, and secreting pleural fluid between them, so facilitating **breathing** movements.

plumule The leafy part of the embryonic **shoot** of **seed** plants. See **germination**.

poikilothermic Describes animals whose body temperatures vary with the temperature of their **environment**. All animals, excluding birds and mammals, are poikilothermic, although often called *cold-blooded*. Compare **homoiothermic**.

pollen Reproductive **cells** of flowering plants, each containing a male **gamete**. Pollen grains are adapted to their mode of transfer, either by insects or by wind.

(a)   air bladders   (b)

pollen (a) Spiky and sticky for insect pollination. (b) Smooth and light for wind pollination.

pollination The transfer of **pollen** grains from **stamens** to **carpels** in flowering plants. Pollination within the same **flower** or between flowers on the same plant is called *self-pollination*. Pollination between two separate plants is called *cross-pollination*. Normally male and female parts of the same plant do not mature simultaneously, favouring cross-pollination with a consequent mixing of **chromosomes**, which can lead to **variation**. Pollen is transferred on the bodies of insects or by the wind. Flowers are adapted to favour one particular method of transfer.

(a) *Insect pollination* Insects visit flowers to drink or collect nectar, attracted by the colour or scent of the flower. Their bodies become dusted with pollen, some of which may adhere to the **stigmas** of subsequent flowers which they visit.

(b) *Wind pollination* Pollen grains carried by the wind must be produced in much higher numbers to compensate for loss during transfer. See **fertilization**, **flowers**, **pollen**.

pollution   The addition of any substance to the **environment** which upsets the natural balance. Pollution has resulted mainly from industrialization which is largely based on *fossil fuel* burning and which caused migration from the land to towns and cities.

(a) Air pollution is caused particularly by fossil fuel burning.

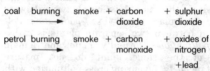

Air pollutants such as smoke and sulphur dioxide cause irritation in the human respiratory system and may accelerate diseases such as bronchitis and lung cancer.

(b) Water pollution results from the intentional or accidental addition of materials into both freshwater and seawater. The pollutants originate from industrial and agricultural practices and also from the home. For example, mine and quarry washings, **acids**, **pesticides**, oil, radioactive wastes, **fertilizers**, detergents, sewage, hot **water** (from power stations). Some pollutants, such as pesticides, may poison aquatic organisms while organic pollutants, such as sewage, cause an increase in the **microorganism** population in the water with a resulting decrease in *dissolved oxygen* levels, making the water unfit for many organisms.

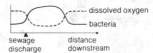

pollution The effect of sewage discharge on oxygen levels in water.

polyploidy A **mutation** in which an organism has extra sets of **chromosomes**. Polyploidy is more common in plants than in animals and often confers advantages, e.g. increased disease resistance.

polysaccharides **Carbohydrates** consisting of long chains of **monosaccharides** linked together by bonds. **Glucose** units can be linked in different ways to form several polysaccharides, such as **starch**, **glycogen** and **cellulose**.

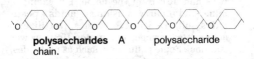

polysaccharides A   polysaccharide
chain.

pooter A device used to collect small insects by using suction.

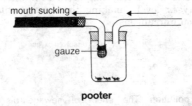

mouth sucking

gauze

pooter

population A group of organisms of the same **species** within a **community**.

posterior Describes parts of the body at or near the hind end of an animal. Compare **anterior**.

predator An animal that feeds on other animals which are called the **prey**, i.e. a predator is a **food consumer** (but is not a **parasite**). The relationship between predator and prey can have dramatic effects on their numbers.

predator A typical predator-prey
relationship.

pregnancy or **Gestation period** In mammals the
time from **conception** to **birth**. Human pregnancy lasts about 40 weeks, the **embryo** developing in the **uterus** after **implantation**. Finger-
like structures (**villi**) grow from the embryo and
develop into the **placenta**.

During pregnancy the cells of the embryo continually divide and differentiate, and the growing embryo (**foetus**) becomes suspended in a
water sac, the **amnion**. The placenta extends
into the **umbilical cord** which connects with the
abdomen of the foetus.

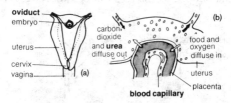

pregnancy (a) Implanted embryo. (b)
Relationship between uterus and placenta.

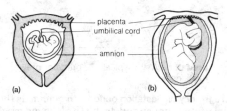

pregnancy (a) Human foetus after twenty weeks. (b) Human foetus just before birth.

premolars Teeth found in front of **molars**.

prey An animal hunted for food by another animal. See **predator**.

primary growth (or *apical growth*) The increase in length and complexity of flowering plant **roots** and **shoots**, as the result of **cell division**, cell

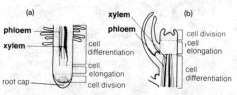

primary growth (a) Root tip. (b) Shoot tip.

elongation and **cell differentiation**, at the root and shoot tips (growth points or **meristems**).

primary sexual characteristics Features which distinguish between males and females from the time of birth but excluding those which develop at **puberty** and are characteristic of adulthood. Compare **secondary sexual characteristics**.

progeny The offspring of **reproduction**.

progesterone A **hormone** secreted by mammalian **ovaries**, which prepares the **uterus** for **implantation** and prevents further **ovulation** during **pregnancy**.

propagation See **vegetative reproduction**.

proprioreceptor A **receptor** which is stimulated by change in position of the body, e.g. stretch receptors in muscle fibres.

protease Any **enzyme** which breaks down **protein** into **peptides or amino acids**, by **hydrolysis**, for example, **pepsin** and **trypsin**.

proteins Organic compounds containing the elements carbon, hydrogen, oxygen and nitrogen and consisting of long chains of subunits called **amino acids**. These chains may then be combined with others, and folded in several different ways, with various types of chemical bonding between chains and parts of chains, giving very large and complex molecules.

Proteins are the 'building blocks' of **cells** and **tissues** being important constituents of **muscle**, **skin**, **bone**, etc. Proteins also play a vital role as **enzymes** while some **hormones** are protein in structure. See **amino acids**, **peptide**.

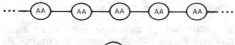

where (AA) = amino acid

proteins Amino acid chains combine to form large and complex molecules.

protein synthesis The synthesis of protein **molecules** from their constituent **amino acids**. The information for the construction of a protein with the correct sequence of amino acids is carried in the arrangement of nitrogen base pairs in **DNA**. This **genetic code** is transcribed exactly into **RNA**. (See diagrams, pages 214, 215.) The first stage is the unzipping of a DNA molecule.

Assume that the N-base sequence of the upper strand is to be transcribed. **Nucleotide** raw materials bond to the appropriate N-base along the DNA strand.

The finished RNA molecule separates from the DNA which has acted as a template. The specific DNA code is now imprinted on the RNA molecule in the form of the corresponding bases. This code represents the information required for protein synthesis. The genetic code 'names' each amino acid by a sequence of 3 adjacent N-bases in DNA and then RNA. These *triplet codes* have been identified for the 20 to 24 amino acids found in living organisms.

The RNA containing the coded triplets is called **messenger RNA**. mRNA molecules move towards and line up at **ribosomes**. Available in the **cytoplasm** are the amino acids and another type of RNA called **transfer RNA**.

Each tRNA molecule is a comparatively short polynucleotide at each end of which is an important N-base triplet. At one end, the 'carrier' end, all tRNA molecules have the same triplet: ACC and this end links with an amino acid. The other end, the 'recognition' end, has a triplet which is specific for a particular amino acid, e.g. the amino acid valine has the specific triplet CAA.

When the tRNA arrives at a ribosome, the specific triplet will be able to bond only to a corresponding triplet along mRNA. In this way, amino acids become positioned along mRNA in a code-determined sequence. By the formation of **peptide** bonds between adjacent amino acids, polypeptides and hence proteins are synthesized.

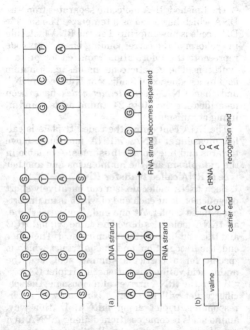

(a)

RNA strand becomes separated

DNA strand

RNA strand

(b)

recognition end

tRNA

carrier end

valine

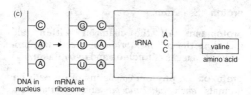

protein synthesis (a) RNA separates from DNA. (b) A tRNA molecule. (c) tRNA bonds with mRNA at a ribosome.

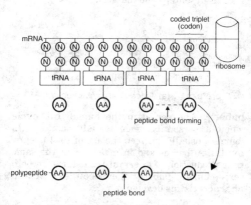

protein synthesis Amino acids bond at a ribosome to form polypeptides.

proton See **atom**.

protoplasm All the material within and including the *cell membrane* of a cell, i.e., protoplasm consists of **nucleus** and **cytoplasm**.

protozoa A **phylum** consisting of **unicellular** animals such as *Amoeba* and *Paramecium*. Protozoans live in a wide variety of **habitats** including stagnant water and **faeces**. They feed on **bacteria** and some cause disease in humans, such as dysentery and malaria.

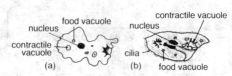

protozoa   (a) *Amoeba*. (b) *Paramecium*.

puberty The period in the human **life cycle** when a person becomes sexually mature. In females, usually between the age of 10–14 years, **ovulation** begins and in males about the same time production of **spermatozoa** starts. In both sexes, during puberty the **secondary sexual characteristics** develop.

pulmonary Describes **organs**, **tissues** and parts of the body related to the **lungs** and

breathing.

pulmonary artery See **pulmonary vessels**, **heart**, **circulatory system**.

pulmonary vein See **pulmonary vessels**, **heart**, **circulatory system**.

pulmonary vessels In mammals, **blood vessels**, which because of their special functions, disagree with the general rule that **arteries** carry oxygenated blood, and **veins** carry deoxygenated blood. The *pulmonary artery* carries deoxygenated blood from the right **ventricle** to the **lungs**, and the *pulmonary vein* carries oxygenated blood from the lungs to the left **atrium**. See **heart**, **circulatory system**.

pulse rate The regular beating in **arteries** due to rhythmic movement of **blood** resulting from **heartbeat**. Pulse rate can be detected in the human body where an artery is close to the skin surface, for example, at the wrist. In an adult human, pulse rate varies from about 70 beats per minute at rest, to over 100 beats per minute during exercise.

punnet square A graphic method used in **genetics** to calculate the results of all possible **fertilizations** and hence the **genotypes** and

phenotypes of **progeny**. In a punnet square, the symbols used to represent one of the parent's **gamete** genotypes are written along the top and those of the other parent down the side. The permutations possible during fertilization are worked out by matching male and female gametes. See **monohybrid inheritance**, **backcross**, **incomplete dominance**.

pupa   A stage in the **life history** of some insects between **larva** and **imago**, during which a radical change in form occurs. See **metamorphosis**.

pure-breeding   Describing an inherited trait controlled by a **homozygous** pair of **alleles**, and which in successive self-crosses reappears generation after generation. See **monohybrid inheritance**.

pyloric sphincter   The ring of muscles which opens and closes the entry to the **stomach**.

pyramid of biomass   A diagram illustrating that organisms at the end of a **food chain** have a smaller total mass (**biomass**). See **pyramid of numbers**.

pyramid of numbers   A diagram illustrating the relationship between members of a **food chain**, showing that the organisms at the end of

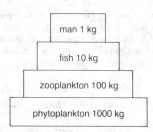

pyramid of biomass The pyramid of biomass in the Antarctic ecosystem.

the chain are usually fewer in number, or to be more exact, have a smaller total mass (**biomass**).

The decrease is caused by **energy** losses at each link in the chain, i.e. each organism in a

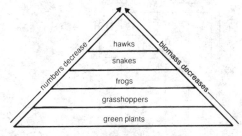

pyramid of numbers

food chain uses up energy in various activities such as heat production and movement. This energy is lost to the subsequent organisms in the chain and so the reduced energy can only support a smaller number of individuals.

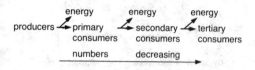

pyramid of numbers

quadrat A square frame used to sample plants

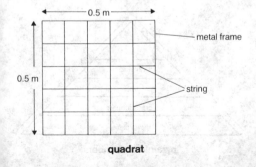

quadrat

(and stationary animals, e.g. barnacles). A quadrat marks off a small area so that the **species** present can be identified and counted. This sample gives an estimate of the numbers and types of species in the whole area. The quadrat must be placed randomly to obtain a representative sample and a number of samples taken.

radicle The embryonic **root** of **seed** plants which is the first structure to emerge from the seed during **germination**. See **germination**.

radius The **anterior** of the two **bones** of the lower region of the **tetrapod** forelimb. In humans, the shorter of the two bones of the forearm. See **endoskeleton**.

receptor or **sense organ** A specialized tissue in an animal which detects **stimuli** from the **environment** and which, by sending **nerve impulses** through the **nervous system**, causes **responses** to be made. See **sensitivity**.

recessive One of a pair of **alleles** which is only expressed in a **homozygous phenotype**. The converse of **dominant**. See **monohybrid inheritance**, **backcross**, **incomplete dominance**.

rectum The terminal part of the vertebrate **intestine** in which **faeces** are stored prior to expulsion via the **anus** or **cloaca**. See **digestion**.

red blood cell or **red blood corpuscle** or **erythrocyte** The most numerous **cell** of vertebrate **blood**, responsible for transporting oxygen from the **lungs** to the **tissues**. In humans, they are made in **bone** marrow and are biconcave discs, without **nuclei**.

Red blood cells contain **haemoglobin** which combines with oxygen as blood passes through the lungs, forming a compound called *oxyhaemoglobin*. At the tissues, this unstable compound breaks down, thus releasing oxygen to the cells.

A shortage of red blood cells is called *anaemia*.

(a)   (b)

diameter
eight microns   side

red blood cell Shape as seen (a) from above and (b) from the side.

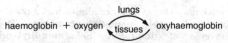

lungs

haemoglobin + oxygen ⇄ tissues → oxyhaemoglobin

red blood cell Haemoglobin delivers oxygen to the tissues.

red blood corpuscle See **red blood cell**.

reflex action A rapid involuntary **response** to a **stimulus**, occurring in most animals and in vertebrates, mediated by the **spinal cord**. Reflex actions can be important in protecting animals from injury, by for instance withdrawing a limb from a hot object.

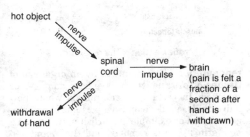

reflex action Path of nerve impulses.

The structures involved and the **nerve impulses** responsible for reflex actions constitute a *reflex arc* which is set up when a nerve impulse is initiated at a receptor. The impulse is transmitted along a sensory **neurone** to the spinal cord where it crosses a **synapse** to a motor neurone.

When a reflex arc operates, nerve impulses are also sent from the spinal cord to the **brain**. Thus, although the response is initiated by the spinal cord, it is through the brain that the animal is aware of what has happened. See **neurones**.

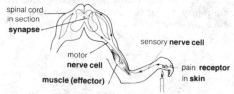

reflex action   The reflex arc.

regeneration   The regrowth by an organism of **tissues** or **organs** which have been damaged or removed. In certain lower animals whole new individuals can develop from portions of a damaged adult. For example, a starfish may develop a new arm if one is removed and the amputated portion may grow a new body.

Regeneration is common among plants. This fact is used by gardeners who grow plants from cuttings. See **artificial propagation**.

In higher animals, this degree of regeneration is not possible, due to the complexity of the **cells** and tissues present in such animals. Thus in mammals, wound healing is the only form of regeneration possible.

renal Describes parts of the body related to the **kidneys** and **urine** production.

reproduction The process by which a new organism is produced from one or a pair of parent organisms. See **asexual reproduction**, **sexual reproduction**.

respiration The reactions by which organisms release the chemical **energy** of food, for example, **glucose**. The energy is used to synthesize **ATP** from *ADP* and is then available for other metabolic processes, for example, **muscle** action.

glucose + oxygen $\longrightarrow$ carbon + water dioxide

$C_6H_{12}O_6 + 6O_2$ ADP ATP $6CO_2 + 6H_2O$

respiration Aerobic respiration.

glucose
$C_6H_{12}O_6$

yeast $\longrightarrow$

ethanol + carbon dioxide
$2CO_2$
$2C_2H_5OH$

ADP ATP

glucose
$C_6H_{12}O_6$

muscle cells $\longrightarrow$

lactic acid
$2CH_3CHOHCOOH$

ADP ATP

respiration Anaerobic respiration.

(a) *Aerobic respiration* Occurs in the presence of oxygen within the **mitochondria** of cells.

(b) *Anaerobic respiration* Occurs in the absence of oxygen within the **cytoplasm** of cells, and provides a lower ATP yield than aerobic respiration.

response   Any change in an organism made in reaction to a **stimulus**. See **sensitivity**.

retina   Light-sensitive **tissue** lining the interior of the vertebrate **eye**, and consisting of two types of **cells** (**rods** and **cones**).

rhizome   An **organ** of **vegetative reproduction** in flowering plants consisting of a horizontal underground stem growing from a parent plant. The tip of the rhizome is a bud from which grows a new plant. Plants which have rhizomes include iris and many types of grass.

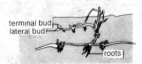

terminal bud
lateral bud

roots

rhizome   A grass rhizome.

rhythmical behaviour   Animal behaviour patterns which are repeated at definite time intervals, e.g. once per day or once per year. Such behaviour is normally triggered by an external **stimulus** such as changes in daylength, and are controlled internally by the animal's **biological clock**. Examples are courtship behaviour, migration and hibernation.

ribosomes Microscopic **cell organelles** in the **cytoplasm** which are the sites of **protein synthesis**.

RNA (ribose nucleic acid) Nucleic acid synthesized by **DNA** in the **nucleus** of cells, and responsible for carrying the **genetic code** from the nucleus into the **cytoplasm** where the synthesis of **proteins** occurs.

RNA differs from DNA in the following ways:
(a) RNA is a single polynucleotide chain;
(b) The sugar group is ribose;
(c) Thymine is replaced by uracil.

rod A light-sensitive **nerve cell** in the **retina** of the vertebrate **eye** which can function in dim light.

root Part of a flowering plant that normally grows down into the **soil**. Its functions are:
(a) absorption of **water** and **mineral salts** from soil;
(b) to anchor the plant in the soil;

(c) in some plants, e.g. turnip, storage of food.

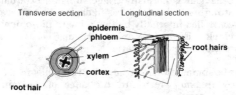

Transverse section   Longitudinal section

epidermis
phloem
xylem
cortex
root hairs
root hair

root The structure of a dicotyledon root.

root cap A cap-shaped layer of **cells**, covering the apex of the growing root tip and protecting it as the root grows through the **soil**.

root tip   root cap
meristem

root cap Longitudinal section through root.

root hairs Tubular projections from **root epidermis cells**, the nucleus usually passing into the hair. Root hairs enormously increase the surface area of the root, and are the principal absorbing **tissue** of the plant. **Water** enters root hairs from the **soil** by **osmosis**, while **mineral salts** are absorbed by **active transport**. The water and mineral salts then pass through the **cortex** cells and enter **xylem** vessels from where they are transported throughout the plant via the **transpiration stream**.

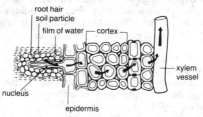

root hairs Water and mineral salts enter the plant via the root hairs.

root nodules Swellings on the roots of *leguminous plants* (for example, clover, bean, pea). Root nodules contain **bacteria** of the **genus** Rhizobium which convert the *nitrogen* of **soil** air into organic nitrogen compounds which can be used by the legumes. This is called **nitrogen fix-**

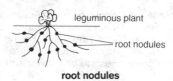

root nodules

ation. See **nitrogen cycle**.

roughage An important component of human **balanced diet**, consisting mainly of the **cellulose** in plant **cell** walls. Although indigestible by man, roughage adds bulk to food and enables the **muscles** of the **alimentary canal** to grip the food and keep it moving by **peristalsis**.

saliva Fluid secreted by *salivary glands* into the **mouths** of many animals in order to moisten and lubricate food. In some mammals, including man, saliva contains the **enzyme** salivary *amylase* (*ptyalin*).

saliva Amylase in saliva digests starch into maltose.

saprophyte An organism that feeds on dead and decaying plants and animals, causing decomposition. Many **fungi** and **bacteria** are saprophytic and play an important role in recycling nutrients. See **carbon cycle**, **nitrogen cycle**.

scapula The dorsal part of the **tetrapod** shoulder girdle. In man, the *shoulder blade*. See **endoskeleton**.

scientific method The procedures by which scientific investigations should be made. Scientific method involves the following steps.

(a) Observation An occurrence is seen to happen on more than one occasion. For example, **starch** in plant **seeds** apparently supplies **energy** during **germination**;

(b) Problem The observation is questioned. For example, how does starch which is a long chain **carbohydrate** become suitable as a respiratory **substrate**?

(c) **Hypothesis** The suggestion of a possible solution. For example, an **amylase enzyme** within seeds degrades starch to **glucose**;

(d) *Experimental* Test the hypothesis. For, example, add seed extract to starch, and test for glucose;

(e) **Theory** The proposal of a solution to the problem based on experimental evidence. For example, in plant seeds, an amylase enzyme degrades starch to glucose which then acts as a respiratory substrate during germination.

All valid scientific investigations follow the guidelines of the scientific method and must include **control experiments** which are identical to the test experiment in all aspects except one. The control provides a standard with which the test experiment can be compared, by showing that any change occurring in the test experiment was due to the factor missing from the control and would not have happened anyway. For example, in the seed/starch experiment, a tube containing starch alone would be a suitable control.

sclerotic The external protective layer of the vertebrate eyeball. See **eye**.

secondary growth or **secondary thickening** The increase in girth which occurs in woody flowering plants each year due to the activity of the **meristem** called **cambium**, which lies between **xylem** and **phloem**.

Further cambium activity produces new xylem and phloem cells, while epidermis becomes bark.

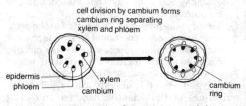

cell division by cambium forms
cambium ring separating
xylem and phloem

epidermis
phloem
xylem
cambium
cambium ring

secondary growth Secondary growth in a woody stem.

Each year a new ring of xylem is added called the *annual ring*. The girth of the plant increases, pushing the phloem and cambium ring outwards, the central core of pith cells being squashed out of existence. The yearly addition of xylem (wood) is called an *annual ring*.

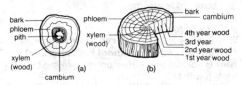

secondary growth (a) A one-year-old stem. (b) A four-year-old stem.

secondary sexual characteristics Features which distinguish between adult male and female animals (excluding **gonads** and associated structures). The development of such features, for example, lion's mane, stag's antlers, and in humans, breast development in females, facial hair in males, etc., is usually controlled by sex **hormones**. Compare **primary sexual characteristics**.

seed The structure that develops from an **ovule** after **fertilization** in flowering plants, and which grows into a new plant. Seeds are enclosed

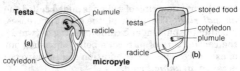

seed The structure of a seed. (a) Broad bean. (b) Maize grain.

within a **fruit**.
Within the seed, the **embryo** becomes differentiated into an embryonic **shoot** bud (**plumule**) and **root** (**radicle**) and either one or two seed leaves (**cotyledons**).
See **fruit and seed dispersal**, **germination**.

selective breeding See **artificial selection**.

selectively permeable membrane Membranes are living structures found surrounding **cells** and bordering regions within cells. They are made up of orderly arrangements of **protein** and **fat molecules**. Certain small molecules may pass through pores in the membrane but larger ones are held back. For this reason the membrane is described as selectively or *semipermeable*. See **cell**, **osmosis**.

semicircular canals Tubes within the vertebrate inner **ear**, which are important in maintaining balance. See **ear**.

sense organ See **receptor**, **sensitivity**.

sensitivity or **irritability** The ability of living organisms to respond to changes in environmental **stimuli**, such as heat, light, sound, etc. Sensitivity enables organisms to be aware of changes in their environment and thus to make appropriate **responses** to any changes that may occur. Certain parts of animals, for example, **eyes**, **ears**, **skin**, are sensitive to particular environmental stimuli and are called **sense organs** or **receptors**. Similarly, plant **tissues** such as **shoot** tips, are receptors, being important in **tropisms**.

As a result of stimuli from the environment, responses are initiated in specialized structures called **effectors**, for example, **muscles**. The responses made by an organism constitute its behaviour.

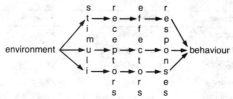

sensitivity Organisms respond to changes in their environment.

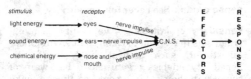

sensitivity A stimulated receptor sends a nerve impulse to the CNS which transmits a response.

In mammals the **receptors** are specialized **cells** connected to the **brain** or **spinal cord** which together make up the **central nervous system** (CNS). In response to a stimulus, the receptors initiate a **nerve impulse** which is transmitted by **nerve cells** to the CNS, i.e. the receptor converts the **energy** of the stimulus into the *electrical energy* of the nerve impulse.

Sense	Stimulus	Receptor
smell	chemicals	nose
taste	chemicals	mouth
touch	contact	skin
hearing	sound	ears
sight	light	eyes
balance	change of position	inner ear

See **ear**, **eye**, **skin**, **smell**, **taste**.

sewage disposal The treatment of sewage in order to make it harmless. Sewage, which is mainly domestic waste, is first piped into tanks where large solids settle out. The remaining liquid is aerated to encourage the growth of **aerobic bacteria** which feed on dissolved organic matter. The **bacteria** are, in turn, eaten by larger organisms and when the dead organisms are allowed to settle, the remaining liquid can now be safely discharged into a river.

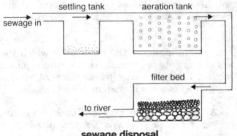

sewage disposal

sex chromosome Any chromosome that is involved in **sex determination**. In **diploid** human **cells** there are 46 chromosomes made up of 23 **homologous chromosome** pairs, one of the pairs being described as sex chromosomes. In the female, the two sex chromosomes are similar and are called X chromosomes. The female **genotype** is thus XX (*homogametic*). In the male, one of the pair is distinctly smaller, and is called the Y chromosome. The male genotype is thus XY (*heterogametic*).

The male is not always the heterogametic sex. For example, in birds, the male is XX, and the female is XY, while in some insects the female is XX and the male is XO, the Y chromosome being absent.

The sex chromosomes, as well as determining sex, also contain **genes** controlling other traits, resulting in what is known as **sex linkage**.

sex determination The method by which the sex of a **zygote** is determined, the most common method being by **sex chromosomes**. Consider the **genotypes** of a human male and female: That is:

(a) A Y-bearing sperm may fertilize an ovum giving a zygote genotype XY and **phenotype** male;

(b) An X-bearing sperm may fertilize an ovum giving a zygote genotype XX and phenotype female. Since half the sperms are X and half are Y, there is an equal chance of the zygote being male or female.

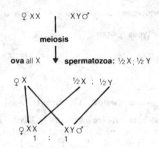

sex determination

sex linkage The presence of **genes** unconnected with sexuality, on a **sex chromosome**, resulting in certain traits appearing in only one sex. In humans, most sex-linked genes are carried on X chromosomes, the Y chromosome being concerned mainly with sexuality.

Example:
The gene for colour blindness in humans is carried on the X chromosome. Normal vision is **dominant** to colour blindness.

If N=normal and n=colour blind:

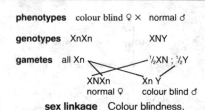

phenotypes   colour blind ♀ × normal ♂

genotypes   XnXn   XNY

gametes   all Xn   ½XN ; ½Y

XNXn   Xn Y
normal ♀   colour blind ♂

sex linkage   Colour blindness.

In this case, the **heterozygous** ♀ XNXn is called a 'carrier' since she has normal vision but carries the **recessive allele**. Thus if crossed with a normal male:

	carrier ♀	×	normal ♂
	XNXn		XNY
gametes	½XN; ½Xn		½XN; ½Y

sperms

		XN	Y
ova	XN	XNXN	XNY
	Xn	XNXn	XnY

Progeny

genotypes   XNXN   XNXn
phenotypes   normal ♀   carrier ♀

genotypes   XNY   XnY
phenotypes   normal ♂   colour blind ♂

sex linkage   The inheritance of colour blindness from a carrier.

That is, the result from the **punnet square** indicates a possibility that half the sons will be colour blind, and half the daughters will be carriers.

A more serious sex-linked trait is **haemophilia** (prolonged bleeding) but its transmission and inheritance is the same as above.

sexual reproduction Reproduction involving the joining or fusing of two sex cells (**gametes**) one from a male parent, and one from a female parent. Gametes are **haploid** and when they fuse (**fertilization**), the resulting composite cell (**zygote**) has the **diploid** number of **chromosomes**. After **fertilization**, the diploid zygote divides repeatedly, ultimately resulting in a new organism. The diagram shows this for humans, who have 46 chromosomes.

Unlike **asexual reproduction**, the offspring of sexual reproduction are genetically unique (except for identical twins) because they obtain half their chromosomes from their male parent and half from their female parent. Thus each

sexual reproduction Two haploid gametes fuse to form a diploid zygote.

fertilization produces a new combination of chromosomes which in turn produce a new organism which will likewise produce gametes by **meiosis**.

shoot That part of a flowering plant which is above **soil** level, for example, **stem**, **leaves**, buds, **flowers**.

short sight (or **myopia**) A human eye defect, mainly caused by the distance from **lens** to **retina** being longer than normal. This results in distant objects being focused in front of the retina giving blurred vision. Short sight is corrected by wearing diverging (concave) lenses.

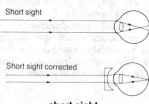

Short sight

Short sight corrected

short sight

skeleton The hard framework of an animal which supports and protects the internal organs. See **endoskeleton**, **exoskeleton**.

skin The layer of **epithelial cells**, **connective**

tissue and associated structures, that covers most of the body of vertebrates.

Mammalian skin consists of two main layers:

(a) The **epidermis**: the outer layer consisting of:
  (i) Cornified layer. Dead cells forming a tough protective outer coat.
  (ii) Granular layer. Living cells which ultimately form the cornified layer.
  (iii) Malpighian layer. Actively dividing cells which produce new epidermis.

(b) The **dermis**: a thicker layer containing **blood capillaries**, hair follicles, sweat glands and **receptor** cells sensitive to touch, heat, cold, pain, pressure.

Beneath the dermis, there is a layer of **fat** storage cells which also act as heat insulation.

The functions of mammalian skin are:

(a) Protects against injury and **microorganism** entry;

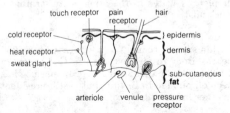

skin Section through mammalian skin.

(b) Reduces **water** loss by evaporation;
(c) Acts as **receptor** for certain environmental **stimuli**;
(d) In **homoiothermic** animals, it is important in **temperature regulation**.

small intestine The **anterior** region of the vertebrate **intestine**. In man, it consists of the **duodenum** (about thirty centimetres in length) and the **ileum** (about seven metres in length). The duodenum receives food from the **stomach**. See **digestion**.

smell The ability of animals to detect odours. In humans, the **receptor cells** involved are in the nasal cavity, and are sensitive to chemical **stimuli**. See **sensitivity**.

smog A harmful side-effect from smoke **pollution** caused by particles of smoke sticking to droplets of water in the atmosphere forming a thick mist.

smoke+fog→smog

Such a smog is thought to have resulted in 4000 deaths from respiratory disease in London in 1952. Since the Clean Air Act of 1956, smog has been eliminated in Britain, but is still prevalent in other industrialized countries.

smoking To smoke tobacco usually in the form

of cigarettes. Smoking is habit-forming and can cause **lung** cancer, bronchitis, and other serious diseases.

smooth muscle See **involuntary muscles**.

soil The weathered layer of the earth's crust intermingled with living organisms and the products of their decay.

The components of soil are:

(a) Inorganic particles (weathered rocks);
(b) **Water**;
(c) **Humus**;
(d) Air;
(e) **Mineral** salts;
(f) **Microorganisms**;
(g) Other organisms (for example, earthworms).

Soil is important because:

(a) It is a **habitat** for a wide variety of organisms;
(b) It provides plants with water and mineral salts;

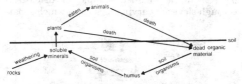

soil Dead organic material is broken down in the soil.

(c) Decomposition of dead organisms in soil releases minerals which can be used by other living organisms.

soil depletion The loss of **mineral salts** from soil when a crop is harvested, which like **soil erosion** may render the soil infertile. Soil depletion can be prevented by
(a) **crop rotation**;
(b) addition of **fertilizers**.

soil erosion The loss of **mineral salts** from soil due to the agricultural practices associated with crop growing, for example, repeated ploughing, deforestation, etc., which make the mineral-rich top soil less stable and more vulnerable to the effects of wind and rain. See **soil depletion**.

soil sieve A device used to separate the four types of inorganic particles in **soil**. The proportion of these particles in a soil can be measured by passing a weighed sample of dried soil through sieves of varying mesh size which separ-

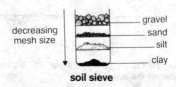

decreasing mesh size

— gravel
— sand
— silt
— clay

soil sieve

ate the particles by size. The separated particles are weighed and their percentage of the complete sample can be calculated. See **soil texture**.

soil texture The types and proportions of inorganic particles in **soil**, of which four types are recognised, based on size.

| clay | salt | sand | gravel |

→ increasing particle size

Soil texture has important effects on soil properties such as water retention and aeration. See **soil types**.

soil thermometer A celsius thermometer adapted for measuring **soil** temperature.

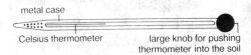

metal case

Celsius thermometer

large knob for pushing thermometer into the soil

soil thermometer

soil types Numerous types of soil exist, but a simple classification recognizes three distinct types:
(a) Sandy (light) **soil** has a high proportion of the

larger inorganic particles, and hence larger air spaces. Thus, sandy soil is well aerated and has good drainage but tends to lose **mineral salts** which are washed downwards (**leaching**).

(b) Clay (heavy) soil has a high proportion of small particles, which means that it retains minerals, but is poorly aerated and can become waterlogged.

(c) Loam soil is the most fertile soil, consisting of a balance of particle types and a good **humus** content. Soils of this type are well-aerated and drain freely, but still retain water and minerals.

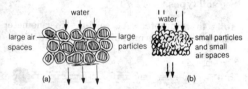

soil types　　(a) Sandy soil. (b) Clay soil.

solution　The mixture (usually a liquid) formed when one substance (the *solute*) dissolves in another (the *solvent*).

> i.e. solute + solvent → solution
> e.g. sugar + water → sugar solution

species　A unit used in the **classification** of

living organisms. It is a group of organisms which share the same general physical characteristics and which can mate and produce fertile offspring. For example, all dogs, despite variation in shape, size etc., are of the same species, but horses and donkeys are separate species within the same **genus**.

spermatozoon or **sperm** Small motile male **gamete** formed in animal **testes**, and usually having a **flagellum**. Sperms are relased from the male in order to fertilize the female gamete. See **fertilization**, **meiosis**.

nucleus

flagellum

spermatazoon

sphincter A ring of **muscle** around tubular **organs**, which by contracting, can narrow or close the passage within the organ.

Examples are the anal sphincter (at the **anus**), and the **pyloric sphincter**. See **digestion**.

spinal cord That part of the vertebrate **central nervous system** which is enclosed within and protected by the backbone.

The spinal cord is a cylindrical mass of **nerve cells** which connect with the **brain** and also with other parts of the body via spinal nerves. The spinal cord consists of three regions:

(a) An inner layer of grey matter consisting of **neurone** cell bodies;

(b) An outer layer of white muscle consisting of nerve fibres running the length of the cord;

(c) A fluid-filled central canal.

The spinal cord conducts **nerve impulses** to and from the brain and is also involved in **reflex actions**.

spinal cord Section showing the three regions.

spiracle One of many pores in the **cuticle** of insects, connecting the **tracheae** with the atmosphere. See **gas exchange**.

spleen An **organ** in the **abdomen**, near the **stomach**, in most vertebrates. It produces **white**

blood cells, destroys worn out **red blood cells**, and filters foreign bodies from the **blood**.

spongy mesophyll Tissue in a **leaf** situated between the **palisade mesophyll** and the lower **epidermis**. Spongy mesophyll **cells** are loosely packed, being separated by air spaces which allow **gas exchange** between the leaf and the atmosphere via the **stomata**. See **leaf**.

spore A reproductive unit, usually microscopic, consisting of one or several **cells**, which becomes detached from a parent organism and ultimately gives rise to a new individual. Spores are involved in both **asexual** and **sexual reproduction** (as **gametes**) and are produced by certain plants, **fungi**, **bacteria** and **protozoa**. Some spores form a resistant resting stage of a **life history** while others allow rapid colonization of new **habitats**.

spore release in the bread mould
Mucor.

sporophyte A phase in the **life history** of a plant that produces **spores**. In plants that show **alternation of generations** it may or may not be the dominant phase. It arises from the **diploid zygote**.

stamen The male part of a **flower** in which **pollen** grains are produced. Each stamen consists of a stalk (filament) bearing an anther. See **anther**.

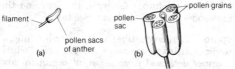

filament

pollen grains

pollen sac

pollen sacs of anther

(a)   (b)

stamen   (a) Stamen. (b) Anther cut open.

starch A **polysaccharide carbohydrate** consisting of chains of **glucose** units and important as an **energy** store in plants. Starch is synthesized during **photosynthesis** and is readily converted to glucose by **amylase enzymes**. See **polysaccharides**.

stem That part of a flowering plant that bears the buds, **leaves**, and **flowers**. Its functions are:
(a) transport of **water**, **mineral salts** and **carbohydrate**;
(b) to raise the leaves above the **soil** for maximum air and light;
(c) to raise the **flowers**, and thus aid **pollination**;
(d) in green stems, **photosynthesis**.

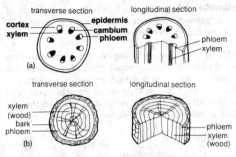

transverse section   longitudinal section

cortex   **epidermis**
xylem   **cambium**
phloem

phloem
xylem

(a)

transverse section   longitudinal section

xylem
(wood)
bark
phloem

phloem
xylem
(wood)

(b)

stem Structure of the stem of a dicotyledonous plant. Transverse and longitudinal sections of (a) a young stem (b) an older stem.

sterilization 1. A procedure to make an organism incapable of **reproduction**.
2. A procedure to make free of **microorganisms**. See **autoclave**.

sternum (or **breastbone**) **Bone** in the middle of the **ventral** side of the **thorax** of **tetrapods**, to which most of the ventral ribs are attached. See **endoskeleton**.

stigma A sticky structure in a flower which traps incoming pollen during **pollination**. See **fertilization**.

stimulus Any change in the **environment** of an organism which may provoke a **response** in the organism. See **sensitivity**.

stolon An **organ** of **vegetative reproduction** in flowering plants consisting of a horizontal **stem** growing from a bud on the parent organism's stem. Stolons grow above the **soil** and eventually the tip becomes established in the soil and develops into an independent plant.

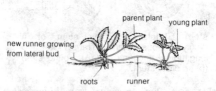

parent plant   young plant

new runner growing
from lateral bud

roots   runner

stolon A strawberry runner is an example of a stolon.

stoma(ta) One of many small pores in the **epidermis** of plants, particularly **leaves**. The evaporation of water during **transpiration**, and **gas exchange**, occur via the stomata. See **guard cells**.

stomach The muscular sac in the **anterior** region of the **alimentary canal**.

In vertebrates, food is passed to the stomach by **peristalsis** via the **oesophagus**.

In the stomach, food is mechanically churned by the peristaltic action of the walls and **protein digestion** is initiated.

In **herbivores**, the stomach has several chambers for **cellulose** digestion.

From the stomach, food is passed into the **small intestine** through the **pyloric sphincter**. See **pepsin**.

striated muscle See **voluntary muscles**.

substrate A substance which is acted upon by an **enzyme**.

sugars **Water** soluble, sweet-tasting crystalline **carbohydrates**, which include the **monosaccharides** and the **disaccharides**.

surface area/volume ratio The ratio

$$\frac{\text{surface area}}{\text{volume}} \quad \text{or} \quad \frac{\text{surface area}}{\text{mass}}$$

is significant to living organisms in several ways. It is difficult to measure the surface area and volume of a plant or animal, but by using cubes as model organisms, the importance of the ratio can be seen. As the object becomes larger, its surface area becomes smaller relative to its volume. In living organisms this ratio has special significance in terms of heat and **water** loss.

(a) Surface area/volume, and heat loss: heat is lost more rapidly from small animals because their relatively larger surface area allows easier heat loss to the air with the following consequences:

  (i) Small mammals such as mice eat relatively more food than larger mammals in order to generate **energy** to replace their high heat losses;

  (ii) Very small birds and mammals are restricted to warm climates;

  (iii) Birds and mammals in cold **habitats** are usually larger than the same **species** living in warm climates.

(b) Surface area/volume, and water loss: relative to their volume, small organisms have a larger evaporating surface and thus a greater tendency to lose water. This is important

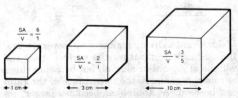

surface area/volume ratio

since many animals and plants have problems controlling water balance so the smaller the organism the greater the problem.

suspensory ligaments Structures holding the **lens** in place in the vertebrate **eye**. See **eye**, **accommodation**.

symbiosis A relationship between organisms of different **species** for the purpose of nutrition. Examples of symbiosis include **parasitism**, **mutualism** and **commensalism**, although the term is sometimes restricted to **mutualism**.

synapse A microscopic gap between the **axon** of one **neurone** and the **dendrites** of another, across which a **nerve impulse** must pass. Nerve impulses arriving at a synapse cause **diffusion** of a chemical substance which crosses the gap initiating nerve impulses in the next neurone.

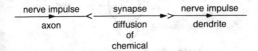

synapse A chemical substance diffuses across the synapse and initiates nerve impulses in the next nerve cell.

synovial membrane Membrane of **connective tissue** lining the capsule of a vertebrate moveable **joint**, being attached to the **bones** at either side of the joint.

The synovial membrane secretes *synovial fluid* which bathes the joint cavity, lubricating the joint when the bones move and cushioning against jarring. See **joint**.

systole See **heartbeat**.

taste The ability of animals to detect flavours. In humans, the **receptor cells** involved are *taste buds* which are sensitive to chemical **stimuli**, and are restricted to the mouth, particularly the tongue. There are four types of taste bud, sensitive to sweetness, sourness, saltiness and bitterness. See **sensitivity**.

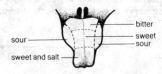

taste A taste map of the tongue.

taxis A locomotory movement of a simple organism or a **cell** in response to an **environmental stimulus**, for example, light.

Such movements show a relationship to the direction of the stimulus, the movement either being towards (positive) or away (negative) from the source of the stimulus.

Taxes are named by adding a prefix which refers to the stimulus. Thus a taxis relative to light is a phototaxis. Examples:

(a) Paramecium is negatively *geotactic*, i.e. it swims away from gravity;
(b) Fruit flies are positively *phototactic*, i.e. they move towards light;
(c) Many **spermatozoa** are positively *chemotactic*, i.e. they move towards chemical substances released by **ova**.

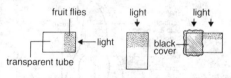

taxis Positive phototaxis in fruit flies.

teeth Structures within the mouth of vertebrates, used for biting, tearing, and crushing food before swallowing.

Enamel A hard substance covering the exposed surface of the tooth (the crown). It contains calcium phosphate and provides an efficient biting surface.

Dentine A substance similar to **bone**, forming the inner part of the tooth.

Pulp Soft **tissue** in the centre of the tooth containing **blood capillaries** which supply food and oxygen, and nerve fibres which register pain if the tooth is damaged.

Root That part of the tooth, within the gum, and embedded in the jawbone by a substance called cement.

The types of teeth are **incisors, canines, premolars, molars** and **carnassials**. See **dental formula, dentition, carnivore, herbivore, omnivore**.

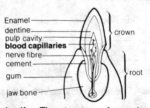

teeth The structure of a tooth.

temperature regulation In **homoiothermic** animals the mechanisms involved in maintaining body temperature within a narrow range (for example, in humans, close to 37°C) so that the normal reactions of **metabolism** can take place.

Some of the temperature regulation methods employed by birds and mammals are outlined below:

(a) Subcutaneous **fat** acts as an insulator;

(b) Hair in mammals and feathers in birds trap air which is a good insulator;

(c) In mammals, evaporation of sweat from the **skin** surface has a cooling effect;

(d) Superficial **blood vessels** constrict (**vasoconstriction**) in response to cold, diverting blood away from the skin surface, and thus reducing heat loss;

(e) Superficial blood vessels dilate (**vasodilation**) in response to heat, bringing blood to the skin surface, from which heat can be lost to the atmosphere.

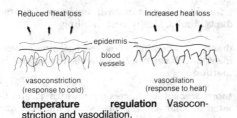

temperature regulation Vasoconstriction and vasodilation.

tendon A band of **connective tissue** by which **muscles** are attached to **bones**.

tensile strength The ability to withstand a certain amount of bending before breaking. See **bone**, **collagen**.

testa The outer protective coat of a **seed** formed from the **integuments** of the **ovule**, after **fertilization**. The testa is usually hard and dry and protects the seed from **microorganisms** and insects.

testcross See **backcross**.

testis The principal reproductive organ in male animals which produces **sperms**. In vertebrates, the paired testes also produce sex **hormones**. See **fertilization**.

tetrapods Vertebrates with two pairs of **pentadactyl limbs**. Mostly land-dwelling.

theory A scientific statement based on experiments which verify a **hypothesis**. See **scientific method**.

thermoreceptor A **receptor** which is stimulated by changes in temperature, e.g. heat and cold receptors in **skin**.

thorax In vertebrates, the part of the body containing **heart** and **lungs** (chest cavity). In mammals, it is separated from the **abdomen** by the **diaphragm**. In insects, the part of the body, **anterior** to the abdomen. See **abdomen**.

thyroid gland An **endocrine gland** in the neck region of vertebrates. When stimulated by *thyroid-stimulating hormone (TSH)* from the **pituitary gland** it produces the **hormone** *thyroxine* which controls the rate of growth and development in young animals.

For example, in tadpoles thyroxine stimulates **metamorphosis**. See **hormones**.

thyroid-stimulating hormone (TSH) See **thyroid gland**.

tibia 1. One of the segments of the insect leg. 2. The **anterior** of the two **bones** in the lower hindlimb of **tetrapods**. In humans, the shinbone. See **endoskeleton**.

tissue In **multicellular** organisms, a group of similar **cells** specialized to perform a specific function. For example, **muscle**, **xylem**.

tissue fluid See **lymph**.

toxin A substance secreted by, for example, bacteria, which is harmful to the organism within which the bacteria are living. See **antibodies**.

trachea **1.** In land vertebrates, the windpipe leading from the **larynx** and carrying air to the **lungs** where it divides into the **bronchi**. The trachea is supported by **cartilage** rings and has a ciliated **epithelium** that secretes **mucus** which traps dust and **microorganisms**. See **lungs**.
2. In insects, one of a branching system of air tubes through which air diffuses into the **tissues** via the **spiracles**. See **gas exchange (insects)**.

transect A line marked off in an area, to study the types of **species** in that area, by sampling the organisms at different points along the line. Measurements of **abiotic factors**, for example, light, **soil pH**, etc., may also be made along the line to discover any relationship between the distribution of particular species and these factors. See **quadrat**.

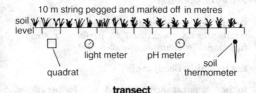

10 m string pegged and marked off in metres

soil level

quadrat   light meter   pH meter   soil thermometer

transect

transfer RNA See **RNA, protein synthesis**.

translocation The transport and circulation of materials within plants. That is:

(a) of water and **mineral salts** in **xylem** vessels via the **transpiration stream**;

(b) of **carbohydrate** produced by **photosynthesis** and conducted through the plant in **phloem** sieve tubes.

transpiration The evaporation of **water** vapour from plant **leaves** via the **stomata**.

transpiration rate **Transpiration** is affected by several environmental factors:

(a) *Temperature* Increased temperature increases water evaporation and thus increases transpiration;

(b) *Humidity* (**water** content of air) Increased humidity causes the atmosphere to become saturated with water, thus reducing transpiration;

(c) *Wind* Increased air movements accelerate transpiration by preventing the atmosphere around **stomata** from becoming saturated with water.

Thus transpiration rate will be greatest in warm, dry, windy conditions. If the rate of water loss by transpiration exceeds the rate of water uptake, **wilting** may occur.

transpiration stream The flow of **water**

through a plant resulting from **transpiration**. Water evaporates through the **stomata**, causing more water to be drawn by **osmosis** from adjacent **leaf cells** (**spongy mesophyll** cells).

The osmotic forces thus set up eventually cause water to be withdrawn from **xylem** vessels in the leaf, resulting in water being pulled through the xylem vessels from the **stem** and **roots**, i.e. water evaporation from leaves causes the flow of water (and **mineral salts**) throughout the plant.

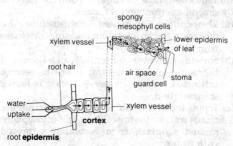

transpiration stream

trophic level In a **food chain**, the level at which a group of organisms occurs. Green plants (producers) are at the lowest level and tertiary consumers (predators) at the highest level.

tropism A plant **growth** movement in response to a **stimulus**, for example, light.

Such movements are related to the direction of the stimulus, the plant **organ** involved growing either towards or away from it. Tropisms are named by adding a prefix which refers to the stimulus.

Examples of tropisms are:

(a) **Geotropism** Response to gravity;

(b) **Phototropism** Response to light;

(c) **Chemotropism** Response to chemicals;

(d) **Hydrotropism** Response to water.

Tropisms can be either positive or negative depending on whether the response is in the same direction as the stimulus or not. See **nastic movement**.

Tropisms are important because they cause plants to grow in such a way that they obtain maximum benefit from the **environment**, in terms of **water**, light, etc.

Tropisms are caused by a plant **hormone** or **auxin** which accelerates growth by stimulating **cell division** and elongation. Uneven distribution of auxin causes uneven growth and leads to bending. See **tropism mechanism**.

tropism mechanism The method by which **tropisms** are controlled by plant **auxins**. The mechanism can be explained by considering experiments done on plant **growth** and **photo-**

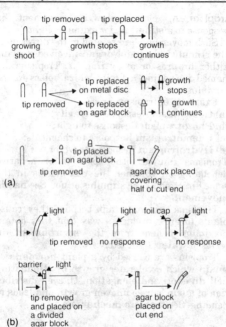

tropism mechanism (a) Shoot tips contain a growth substance. (b) Its action is affected by light.

tropism using growing **shoots**.

A growth substance is produced in shoot tips. This substance diffuses downwards and accelerates growth by stimulating **cell division** and elongation. Uneven distribution of the growth substance results in bending. See diagram (a).

Shoot tips contain cells which are sensitive to light. See diagram below. One-sided light causes the growth substance to diffuse from the illuminated side and accelerate growth at the non-illuminated side. As a result of this uneven growth, the shoot bends towards the light. See diagram (b).

accelerated growth — growth substance — light

tropism mechanism   A shoot tip.

trypsin   A **protease enzyme** secreted by the vertebrate **pancreas**. See **duodenum**.

TSH   See **thyroid-stimulating hormone**.

tuber   An **organ** of **vegetative reproduction** in flowering plants. Tubers can form from **stems** or **roots** and consist of a food store and buds from which develop new plants. See diagram on page 270.

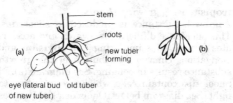

tuber (a) Stem tuber, e.g. potato. (b) Root tuber, e.g. dahlia.

Tullgren funnel An apparatus used to isolate organisms living in the air spaces in **soil**, e.g. beetles and spiders. The organisms move away from strong light and high temperature produced by a lamp and are collected in a jar of preservative.

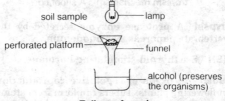

Tullgren funnel

turgor The state of a plant **cell** after maximum

water absorption. Surrounding water enters a cell by osmosis causing the **vacuole** to expand, pushing the **cytoplasm** against the cell wall and making the plant cell solid and strong.

Turgid cells are important in supporting plants, conferring strength and shape. Young plants depend completely on turgor for support, although in older plants, support is obtained from **wood** formation.

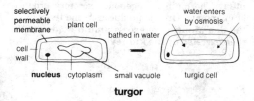

turgor

tympanic membrane   See **tympanum**.

tympanum (or **tympanic membrane**) A thin membrane separating the outer ear and middle ear in tetrapods, i.e. the *eardrum*. See **ear**.

ulna The **posterior** of the two **bones** of the lower region of the **tetrapod** forelimb. In humans, the larger of the two bones of the forearm. See **endoskeleton**.

umbilical cord The cord of blood vessels linking the growing **foetus** in the womb to the **placenta**. It carries nourishment to the foetus and waste products from it. See **birth, pregnancy**.

unicellular (of an organism) Consisting of one cell only. Unicellular organisms include **protozoans, bacteria** and some **algae**. Compare **multicellular**.

urea The main nitrogenous excretory product of mammals. Urea is produced in the **liver** from the **deamination** of excess **amino acids** and is then excreted by the **kidneys**.

$$H_2N-C-NH_2$$
$$\underset{O}{\overset{\parallel}{}}$$

urea The chemical structure of urea.

ureter In vertebrates, the tube carrying **urine** from the **kidney** to the **bladder**. See **kidney**.

urethra The tube in mammals which conveys **urine** from the **bladder** to the exterior. In male mammals, it also serves as a channel for the exit of **spermatazoa**. See **kidney, fertilization**.

uterus (or **womb**) A muscular cavity in most

female mammals that contains the **embryo(s)** during development. The uterus receives **ova** from the **oviduct** and connects to the exterior via the **vagina**. See **fertilization**.

urine A solution of **urea** and **mineral salts** in water produced by the mammalian **kidney**. It is stored in the **bladder** before discharge via the **urethra**.

vaccine A small quantity of **antigens** which is injected into the body. This stimulates the production of the appropriate **antibodies**, which are then present if and when that particular **microorganism** enters the body.

vacuole A fluid-filled space within **cell cytoplasm**, containing many compounds, for example, sugars in solution. Vacuoles are particularly important in maintaining **turgor** in plant cells. See **cell, contractile vacuole**.

vagina A duct in most female mammals which receives the **penis** during **copulation**. It connects the **uterus** with the exterior, and is the route by which the **foetus** is passed during **birth**. See **fertilization**.

valves Membranous structures within animal **circulatory systems** which allow **blood** to flow in one direction only.

(a) *Mitral valve* (or *bicuspid valve*) Two flaps between the left **atrium** and left **ventricle** of the heart in birds and mammals;

(b) *Tricuspid valve* Three flaps between the right atrium and right ventricle of the mammalian heart;

(c) *Semilunar valves* Half-moon shaped flaps in the mammalian heart between the right ventricle and **pulmonary artery**, and the left ventricle and **aorta**. Semilunar valves are also found in the **lymphatic system** and **veins**. See **heart, heartbeat**.

variation Differences in characteristics between members of the same **species**. There are two main types:

(a) *Continuous variations* in which there are degrees of variation throughout the **population** showing **normal distribution** around a mean. For example, in humans: height, weight, **pulse rate**;

(b) *Discontinuous variations* are absolutely clear cut, i.e., there are no intermediate forms, for example, **blood groups** in humans. Discontinuous variations do not show normal distribution and are used when doing **genetics** crosses.

Variation within a species results either from inherited or environmental factors or a combination of both. Thus, a human being inherits **genes** influencing height for example, but will also be subject to environmental factors such as nutrition. Inherited variations are considered to be the basis of **evolution** by **natural selection**.

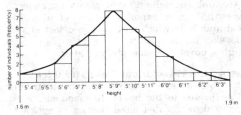

variation Height in men — an example of continuous variation.

vascular bundle A strand of longitudinal conducting **tissue** within plants, consisting mainly of xylem and phloem. See **root, stem, leaf**.

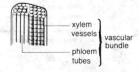

xylem vessels
phloem tubes
} vascular bundle

vascular bundle A vascular bundle in a stem.

vasoconstriction See **temperature regulation**.

vasodilation See **temperature regulation**.

vegetative reproduction (or **propagation**) **Asexual reproduction** in plants by an outgrowth from a parent organism of a **multicellular** body which may become detached and develop independently into a new plant. See **bulbs, corm, rhizome, stolon, tuber**.

vein 1. A **vascular bundle** in a plant leaf.
2. A **blood vessel** which transports **blood** from the **tissues** to the **heart**. In mammals, veins carry deoxygenated blood (for an exception to this rule, see **pulmonary vessels**) and form from smaller vessels called *venules* which carry blood from the **capillaries**. Veins are thin-walled, and since the **blood pressure** in veins is less than in **arteries**, they have valves to prevent the blood flowing away from the heart.

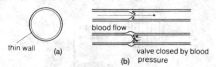

vein (a) Section through a vein. (b) Valve operation in veins.

vena cava The largest **vein** in the **circulatory system** of vertebrates. In mammals, either of the two main veins:

(a) *superior vena cava* carries **blood** from the head, neck and upper limbs into the right **atrium** of the **heart**;

(b) *inferior vena cava* carries **blood** from the rest of the body and lower limbs into the right atrium.

ventral Describes features of, on, or near that surface of an organism which is normally directed downwards, although in humans, it is directed forwards. Compare **dorsal**.

ventricle See **heart**, **heartbeat**.

vertebral column (or **backbone**) A series of closely arranged **bones** (vertebrae) and/or **cartilages** which runs dorsally from the skull to the tail in vertebrates. It is the principal longitudinal supporting structure and encloses and protects the **spinal cord**. See **endoskeleton**.

villi (singular **villus**) 1. Finger-like projections in the vertebrate **intestine** where their large numbers increase the surface area available for **absorption** of food. See **ileum**.
2. Finger-like projections which develop from the mammalian **placenta** into the **uterus** wall and

thus increase the area of contact between maternal and embryonic **tissues**.

virus   The smallest known living particle, having a diameter between 0.025 and 0.25 microns. Viruses are **parasites** infecting animals, plants and **bacteria**. Virus infections of man include measles, polio and influenza.

A virus particle consists of a **protein** coat surrounding a length of **nucleic acid**, either **DNA** or **RNA**.

bacterium
virus becomes
attached to
bacterium

the virus nuclear
material is injected
into the bacterium
and causes the
assembly of new
virus parts

the bacterium cell wall
is ruptured, releasing
many new viruses

virus   A virus infecting a bacterium

viscera   A collective term for the internal **organs** of an animal.

vitamins   **Organic compounds** required in small quantities by living organisms. Like **enzymes**, vitamins play a vital role in chemical reactions within the body, often regulating an enzyme's action. Shortage of vitamins from the human diet leads to *deficiency diseases*.

The properties of some important vitamins are summarized below.

Vitamin A	Rich sources	Effects of deficiency
Vitamin	milk, liver, butter, fresh vegetables	night-blindness, retarded growth
Vitamin B$_1$	yeast, liver	*Beri-beri*: loss of appetite and weakness
Vitamin B$_2$	yeast, milk	*pellagra*: skin infections, weakness, mental illness
Vitamin C	citrus fruits, fresh green vegetables	*scurvy*: bleeding gums, loose teeth, weakness
Vitamin D	eggs, cod liver oil	*rickets*: abnormal bone formation
Vitamin E	fresh green vegetables, milk	thought to affect reproductive ability
Vitamin K	fresh vegetables	blood clotting impaired

vitreous humour A transparent jelly-like material which fills the cavity behind the **lens** of the vertebrate **eye**.

voluntary (striated) muscles Muscles connected to the mammalian **skeleton** and under the conscious control of the organism, for example, the limb muscles, muscles of face and mouth, etc. Voluntary muscles involved in limb movement are attached to **bones** by **tendons** and cause movement by contracting and thus pulling on bones, particularly at **joints**. See **involuntary muscles**, **antagonistic muscles**.

wall pressure A cell absorbing water by **osmosis** will continue to expand until its **selectively permeable membrane** and **cell wall** can stretch no further. The resistance to stretching is known as 'wall pressure' and increases as the point of **turgor** is approached.

warm-blooded See **homoiothermic**.

water A **compound** consisting of the elements hydrogen and oxygen. Its chemical formula is H_2O. **Water** can be synthesized by burning hydrogen in air.

$$\text{hydrogen} + \text{air} \atop \text{(oxygen)} \xrightarrow[\text{energy}]{\text{heat}} \text{water}$$

Water can be split into its two **elements**:

1

$$\text{water} \xrightarrow[\text{energy}]{\text{electrical}} \text{hydrogen} + \text{oxygen}$$

2

$$\text{water} \xrightarrow[\text{energy}]{\text{light}} \text{hydrogen} + \text{oxygen}$$

Reaction **2** occurs in green plants during **photosynthesis**.

Water is a colourless, tasteless compound which freezes at 0°C and boils at 100°C. Water can exist in several states as shown in the water cycle.

Water is biologically important for the following reasons:

(a) Water as a major cell constituent. Water is the most abundant component of organisms. It is estimated that the human body is more than 60% water. The water content of living organisms can be estimated by weighing food samples, e.g. a potato, drying the samples in an oven, and then reweighing. The resulting loss of weight gives the water content.

The water content of living organisms is usually between 60% and 95%, although it can be as high as 99% (jellyfish) and as low as 20% (plant seeds).

(b) Water as a solvent. Water is called 'the universal solvent' since more substances dissolve in water than in any other liquid. This is important, since all the chemical reactions which occur in organisms take place in aqueous solution, i.e. dissolved in water (*aqua*=water).

(c) Transport. Within organisms, substances, e.g. food, are required to be transported throughout the organism. Such materials are transported in aqueous solution e.g. **blood**.

(d) Syntheses. Water is important in the syntheses of many compounds in living organisms, e.g. one of the raw materials for **photosynthesis** is water.

(e) Lubrication. The internal **organs** and **joints** of living organisms must be lubricated to prevent friction during movement. Various lubricating fluids exist, e.g. **mucus**, all of which are aqueous solutions.

(f) Reproduction. Many organisms use water to transport the male **cells** (**sperm**) to the female cells (**ovum**) so that **fertilization** can occur.

(g) Temperature control. The evaporation of water (e.g. sweat) from the surface of organisms has a cooling effect, while the high water content of cells provides insulation and prevents rapid temperature changes.

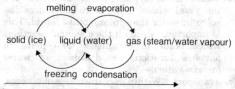

water

water purification The treatment applied to tap water in order to make it safe to drink. The **water** is filtered through sand and gravel to remove large particles and then chlorine is added to kill harmful **microorganisms**.

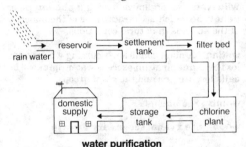

water purification

weathering The process by which exposed rock is converted into **soil**. The rock is broken down to small particles by the effects of wind, rain, heat and frost. These rock particles form the 'skeleton' of the soil but are only one component of a complex mixture of inorganic and organic factors which make up a soil. See **soil**.

white blood cell (or **white blood corpuscle** or **leucocyte**) One of various types of **blood cell** found in most vertebrates. Their function is in defence against **microorganism** infection, which they achieve by **phagocytosis** or by **anti-body** production.

white blood corpuscle   See **white blood cell**.

wild type   An organism having a **phenotype** or **genotype** which is characteristic of the majority of the **species** in natural conditions.

wilting   A plant condition occurring when water loss by **transpiration** exceeds water uptake. The **cells** lose **turgor** and the plant droops.

womb   See **uterus**.

wood   See **xylem**, **secondary growth**.

xylem   **Tissue** within plants which conducts **water** and **mineral salts**, absorbed by **roots** from the **soil**, throughout the plant. Xylem tissue consists of long continuous tubes formed from columns of **cells** in which the horizontal cross walls have disintegrated and the cell contents have died.
The vessels thus formed are strengthened by a compound called **lignin**, and ultimately form the **wood** of the plant. Associated with xylem vessels, and providing additional strength, are specialized cells called xylem fibres, some of which are useful, for example, flax. Thus xylem is com-

mercially important as a source of wood and fibres. See **leaf, root, secondary growth, stem**.

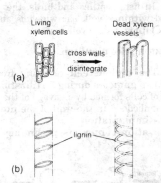

xylem (a) Long continuous vessels are formed as horizontal cross walls disintegrate. (b) The vessels are strengthened by lignin.

yeast A **unicellular fungus** which is important in *baking*, **brewing** and **fermentation**. See **budding**.

yellow spot See **fovea**.

yolk A store of food material, mainly **protein** and **fat** present in the eggs (**ova**) of most animals. In fish, reptiles and birds, the yolk is contained within a yolk sac which is absorbed into the **embryo** as the yolk is used.

zooplankton See **plankton**.

zygote The **diploid cell** resulting from the fusion of two **gametes** during **fertilization**. The tiny ball of cells formed by cleavage of the zygote becomes embedded in the wall of the **uterus** in mammals (**implantation**).
See **fertilization in humans, pregnancy**.

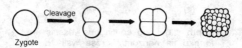

Zygote

Cleavage

zygote The zygote divides by mitosis after fertilization to form a ball of cells.

APPENDIX A: Chemical elements

In this Table, we give the names and symbols of the chemical elements, with their proton numbers (Z), numbers of isotopes (n_i) and melting and boiling temperatures (T_m, T_b).

Element	Z	n_i	$T_m/°C$	$T_b/°C$
Actinium Ac	89	7	1230	3100
Aluminium Al	13	7	660	2400
Americium Am	95	8	1000	2600
Antimony Sb	51	18	631	1440
Argon Ar	18	7	−190	−186
Arsenic As	33	11	—	610
Astatine At	85	7	250	350
Barium Ba	56	16	710	1600
Berkelium Bk	97	6		
Beryllium Be	4	4	1280	2500
Bismuth Bi	83	12	271	1500
Boron B	5	4	2030	3700
Bromine Br	35	18	−7	58
Cadmium Cd	48	18	321	767
Caesium Cs	55	15	27	690
Calcium Ca	20	11	850	1450
Californium Cf	98	7		
Carbon C	6	6	3500	3900
Cerium Ce	58	13	804	2900
Chlorine Cl	17	10	−101	−34
Chromium Cr	24	8	1900	2600
Cobalt Co	27	10	1490	2900
Copper Cu	29	10	1080	2580
Curium Cm	96	7	1340	

Element	Z	n_i	T_m/°C	T_b/°C
Dysprosium Dy	66	12	1500	2300
Einsteinium Es	99	10		
Erbium Er	68	10	1530	2600
Europium Eu	63	12	830	1450
Fermium Fm	100	7		
Fluorine F	9	4	−220	−188
Francium Fr	87	5	30	650
Gadolinium Gd	64	14	1320	2700
Gallium Ga	31	10	30	2250
Germanium Ge	32	13	960	2850
Gold Au	79	13	1060	2660
Hafnium Hf	72	11	2000	5300
Helium He	2	3	−	−269
Holmium Ho	67	6	1500	2300
Hydrogen H	1	3	−259	−253
Indium In	49	19	160	2000
Iodine I	52	17	114	183
Iridium Ir	77	10	2440	4550
Iron Fe	26	8	1539	2800
Krypton Kr	36	19	−157	−153
Lanthanum La	57	8	920	3400
Lawrencium Lw	103	1		
Lead Pb	82	24	327	1750
Lithium Li	3	4	180	1330
Lutetium Lu	71	5	1700	3300
Magnesium Mg	12	6	650	1100
Manganese Mn	25	9	1250	2100
Mendelevium Md	101	1		
Mercury Hg	80	16	−39	357
Molybdenum Mo	42	15	2600	4600
Neodymium Nd	60	13	1020	3100
Neon Ne	10	7	−250	−246

Element	Z	n_i	T_m/°C	T_b/°C
Neptunium Np	93	8	640	3900
Nickel Ni	28	11	1450	2800
Niobium Nb	41	15	2400	5100
Nitrogen N	7	6	−210	−196
Nobelium No	102	1		
Osmium Os	76	13	3000	4600
Oxygen O	8	6	−219	−183
Palladium Pd	46	17	1550	3200
Phosphorous P	15	7	44	280
Platinum Pt	78	12	1770	3800
Plutonium Pu	94	11	640	3500
Polonium Po	84	12	250	960
Potassium K	19	8	63	760
Praseodymium Pr	59	8	930	3000
Promethium Pm	61	8	1000	1700
Protactinium Pa	91	9	1200	4000
Radium Ra	88	8	700	1140
Radon Rn	86	7	−71	−62
Rhenium Re	75	7	3180	5600
Rhodium Rh	45	14	1960	3700
Rubidium Rb	37	16	39	710
Ruthenium Ru	44	12	2300	4100
Samarium Sm	62	14	1050	1600
Scandium Sc	21	11	1400	2500
Selenium Se	34	16	220	690
Silicon Si	14	6	1410	2500
Silver Ag	47	16	960	2200
Sodium Na	11	6	98	880
Strontium Sr	38	13	77	1450
sulphur S	16	7	119	445
Tantalum Ta	73	11	3000	5500
Technetium Tc	43	14	2100	4600

Element	Z	n_i	$T_m/°C$	$T_b/°C$
Tellurium Te	52	22	450	1000
Terbium Tb	65	8	1360	2500
Thalium Tl	81	16	300	1460
Thorium Th	90	9	1700	4200
Thulium Tm	69	10	1600	2100
Tin Sn	50	21	231	2600
Titanium Ti	22	8	1680	3300
Tungsten W	74	10	3380	5500
Uranium U	92	12	1130	3800
Vanadium V	23	7	1920	3400
Xenon Xe	54	22	−111	−108
Ytterbium Yb	70	11	820	1500
Yttrium Y	39	12	1500	3000
Zinc Zn	30	13	420	907
Zirconium Zr	40	12	1850	4400

APPENDIX B: Units of measurement

Length
1 metre (m)=100 centimetres (cm)
1 centimetre=10 millimetres (mm)
1 millimetre=1000 microns (μm)
1 micron=1000 nanometres (nm)

Volume
1 litre (l)=1000 cm^3 (millilitres (ml))

Mass
1 tonne=1000 kilogrammes (kg)
1 kilogramme=1000 grammes (g)

Temperature
boiling point of water=100° Celsius (°C)
freezing point of water=0°C
normal average human body temperature=37°C

Energy
1 kilojoule (kJ)=1000 Joules (J)=240 calories (C)

Food type	Energy value
Carbohydrate	17 kJ/g
Protein	17 kJ/g
Fat	39 kJ/g

APPENDIX C: Characteristics of living things

For an organism to be considered as living it must demonstrate all of the following features:

Movement	The ability to change position either of all, or, of part of the body.
Excretion	The ability to remove from the body waste materials produced by the organism
Respiration	The ability to release energy by the breakdown of complex chemicals.
Reproduction	The ability to produce offspring.
Irritability	The ability to sense and respond to changes in the environment.
Nutrition	The ability to take in or manufacture food that can be used when required as a source of energy or as building materials.
Growth	The ability to increase in size and complexity through the production of new cell material.

APPENDIX D: The differences between plants and animals

Plants	Animals
Cell surrounded by cellulose cell wall	No cellulose cell wall
Large vacuoles in cells filled with cell sap	Vacuoles when present only small
Large cells with definite shape	Small irregularly shaped cells
Only restricted movement possible	Free movement possible
Response to stimulus slow	Rapid response to stimulus
Cells contain chloroplasts (chlorophyll)	No chloroplasts (chlorophyll)
Photosynthesize	Must obtain food from external sources

These characteristic differences should only be regarded as guidelines. Attempts to classify certain organisms within these terms of reference will be difficult and has provided scientists with great problems, for example, Bacteria, Fungi, Viruses.

APPENDIX E: The major groups of living organisms

THE ANIMAL KINGDOM (major phyla)

(a) INVERTEBRATES   Animals   without   a **vertebral column** (backbone)

Phylum Protozoa   Microscopic **unicellular** animals.

Amoeba

Paramecium

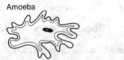

Phylum Porifera Porous animals often occurring in colonies, for example, sponges.

bath sponge

Phylum Coelenterata Tentacle-bearing animals with stinging cells.

Hydra   *Jelly fish*   *Sea anenome*

Phylum Platyhelminthes Flatworms.

Planaria   *Tapeworm*

Phylum Annelida Segmented worms.

Earthworm   *Leech*   *Sandworm*

Phylum Mollusca   Soft-bodied animals often with shells.

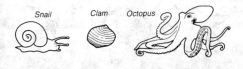

Snail   *Clam*   *Octopus*

Phylum   Arthropoda   Jointed   limbs;
exoskeleton.

Class Insecta (*louse*)   Class Crustacea (*shrimp*)

Class Insecta (*louse*)   Class Crustacea (*shrimp*)

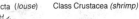

Class Arachnida (*spider*) Class Chilopoda (*centipede*)

Phylum Echinodermata Spiny-skinned marine
animals.

Starfish   *Sea urchin*   *Brittle star*

(b) VERTEBRATES   (Phylum   Chordata)
Animals with a vertebrate column.

Class Pisces (Fish)
Fins, Scales, Aquatic.

Trout

Class Amphibia (amphibians)
moist, scaleless skin, live both
on land and water.

Toad

Class Reptilia (reptiles)
dry scaly skin.

Turtle

Class Aves (birds) feathers,
constant temperature.

Robin

Class Mammalia (mammals)   Hair; constant temperature; young suckled with milk.

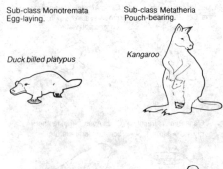

Sub-class Monotremata
Egg-laying.

Duck billed platypus

Sub-class Metatheria
Pouch-bearing.

Kangaroo

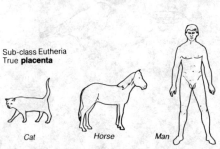

Sub-class Eutheria
True **placenta**

Cat

Horse

Man

SUMMARY

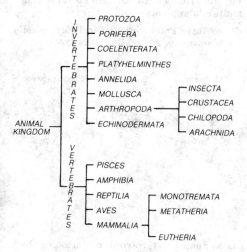

THE PLANT KINGDOM (major phyla)

Phylum Thallophyta Unicellular and simple multicellular plants.

Class Algae Photosynthetic; includes unicellular, filamentous, and multicellular types.

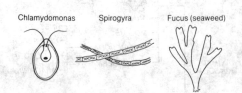

Chlamydomonas   Spirogyra   Fucus (seaweed)

Class Fungi Heterotrophic; including both **parasites** and **saprophytes**.

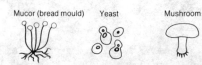

Mucor (bread mould)   Yeast   Mushroom

Phylum Bryophyta Green plants with simple **leaves** and showing **alternation of generations**; moist **habitats**.

Class Hepaticae (liverworts)

Pellia

Funaria

Phylum Pteridophyta (ferns; bracken; horsetails) Green plants, with **roots, stems, leaves,** and showing **alternation of generations**.

Fern

Phylum Spermatophyta **Seed** producing plants.

Class Gymnospermae **Seeds** produced in **cones**.

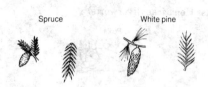

Spruce   White pine

Class Angiospermae Flowering plants; **seeds** enclosed within **fruits**.

monocotyledons
narrow-leaves: one
cotyledon

dicotyledons broad-leaved
two **cotyledons**

Grass   Wheat   Rose   Oak

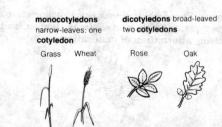

SUMMARY

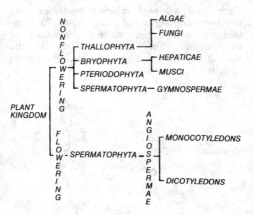

Bacteria and viruses do not meet the criteria necessary to be placed in either the animal or plant kingdoms.

APPENDIX F: How biologists look at things

Terms such as **dorsal, anterior, posterior**, refer to a particular surface of an organism. The location of these areas depends on the orientation of the organism. For example, in the dog, the ventral surface points downwards, whereas in man, it points forwards.

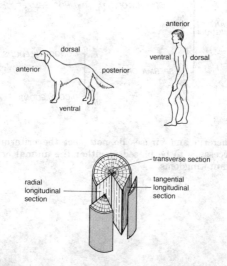

Other terms are used to describe different ways of looking at sections through organisms, for example, transverse and longitudinal.

APPENDIX G: The geological timescale

Era	Period	Beginning (10^6 years ago)
Cenozoic	Quaternary (Q)	1
	Tertiary (Te	55
Mesozoic	Cretaceous (C)	120
	Jurassic (J)	155
	Triassic (Tr)	190
Palaeozoic	Permian (P)	215
	Carboniferous (Car)	300
	Devonian (D)	350
	Silurian (S)	390
	Ordovician (O)	480
	Cambrian (Cam)	550

The occurrence of fossils in relation to this time-scale is shown in the next table.

	Vertebrates	Invertebrates	Plants
Q	Hominids appear	Arthropods, molluscs abundant	
Te	Mammals emerge, dinosaurs extinct	Modern groups emerge	
Cr	Dinosaurs dominant	Ammonoids extinct	Flowering plants emerge
J	Birds emerge	Modern crustacea emerge, ammonoids abundant	
Tr	Reptiles flourish, dinosaurs emerge	Marine forms decline	
P	Amphibia decline	Trilobites extinct	Conifers emerge

	Vertebrates	Invertebrates	Plants
Car	Reptiles emerge		
D	Amphibia emerge, fish abundant	Insects emerge	Mosses, horsetails, ferns emerge
S		Trilobites decline, brachiopods abundant	
O	Fish emerge		First land plants emerge
Cam		Most invertebrate phyla present; trilobites and brachiopods flourish	

The fossil record

APPENDIX H: Biographies

Some people who have made important contributions to our understanding of biology

Crick, Francis (1916–) English molecular biologist who contributed to the discovery of the helical structure of **DNA**.

Darwin, Charles (1809–82) English scientist who formulated the theory of **evolution** by natural selection, expounded in his book *On the Origin of Species* (1859).

Fleming, Sir Alexander (1881–1955) Scottish bacteriologist who discovered **penicillin** (1928).

Harvey, William (1578–1657) English physician who discovered the mechanism of the blood **circulatory system**.

Hill, Robert (1899–1991) English biochemist who in 1936 demonstrated the 'light stage' of **photosynthesis**.

Hopkins, Frederick (1861–1947) English biochemist who in 1906 published reports on experiments involving substances present in food that are needed for healthy growth. These substances were later called **vitamins**.

Koch, Robert (1843–1910) German bacteriologist who discovered the **bacterium** responsible for tuberculosis and contributed much of what was known about cholera and malaria.

Krebs, Sir Hans (1900–81) British biochemist who made important discoveries about the processes involved in cell **respiration**.

Leeuwenhoek, Anton van (1632–1723) Dutch microscopist who made the first drawings of **bacteria** and described the general structure of **yeast** and **red blood cells** for the first time.

Linneaeus, Carl (1707–78) Swedish botanist who established the binomial (two-name) system for the **classification** of animals and plants.

Mendel, Gregor (1822–84) Austrian monk and botanist who founded the science of **genetics** with his experiments on the hybridization of pea plants.

Pasteur, Louis (1822–95) French microbiologist who did pioneering work on **fermentation**, and on **immunization** against diseases such as anthrax and rabies.

Watson, James (1928–) American biologist who contributed to the discovery of the helical structure of DNA.

APPENDIX I: Writing up experiments

Your aim should be to give an account which would enable another scientist to copy precisely your procedure and to draw conclusions from your observations.

The traditional way of reporting an experiment includes:

Title	A summary of the aim or aims.
Introduction	A brief outline of useful background information.
Apparatus	A complete list (or labelled diagram) of everything used.
Method	An ordered account of what was done. (A labelled diagram may help.)
Result	A record of observations and measurement using tables, graphs, diagrams or description.
Discussion and Conclusion	An objective account of what has been learned, problems encountered, and further investigations that arise from the observations.

APPENDIX J: Drawing diagrams

A diagram represents something as simply as possible. You do not have to be an artist to draw one, but you do need to follow a few basic rules:

— Equip yourself with a sharp pencil, a ruler and a rubber.

— Draw diagrams large enough to show detail easily.

— Lines should be single and complete to give a neat outline.

— Lines should complete a structure without leaving holes, going too far or blocking passages.

— The use of colours or shading should only be used to make an important feature stand out.

— Diagrams require a clear title.

— Labels are used to indicate the names of the parts shown.

— Annotations are used to give a brief description of the parts shown.

— Labels and annotations should be arranged horizontally around the outside of the diagram.

— Lines (drawn with a ruler) should precisely connect the labels and annotations to the parts to which they refer.

— Label and annotation lines should never cross each other.

A good diagram is often worth more than a long description.